REVOLUTIONARY POPULAR CULTURE

The cover was designed by Leigh Brownhill, Laura Belanger, Terisa Turner, John Hanson and Timothy Belknap. We thank the artists who produced the original images.

Photo and Graphics Credits

R. Bonanno of the University of Massachusetts *Collegian* took the photographs in "Hands Across the Campus Against Racism." Terisa Turner photographed her students. Seth Tobocman and his colleagues in New York who put out the world's best comic - *World War 3*, contributed many of the graphics. Many other artists and photographers including Peter Magubane and Sam Nzima, produced the famous and less known illustrations used here. We thank them and the International Defense and Aid Fund for Southern Africa.

Revolutionary Popular Culture

This book is a about the new world society emerging from the disarray of the old. The collection came out of a year of self-education by members of the social thought and political economy seminar taught by Terisa Turner.

UNITE

Seth Tobocman

Editors

Matthew J. Collins
Timothy A. Belknap
Leigh Brownhill
Terisa Turner
Laura Belanger
John Hanson

The tasks that the editors undertook varied from writing, taking trips to New York, teaching word processing, taking and processing photographs, organizing potluck dinner work sessions, working the phone tree, and executing logistics. It so happened that we all both decided and did all of these things.

Authors and Contributors

Laura Belanger	Timothy Belknap
Benjamin Bennett	Leigh Brownhill
Janine Cardello	Matthew Collins
Daria Casinelli	Erin Crawley
Taciana Ribero	Jane Devine
C.L.R. James	Terisa Turner
John Hanson	Jim Murray
Seth Tobocman	Melissa Hatrak
Donna Coombs	David Heggestad
Ralph Reed	Rachel Maiore
Amy Pearson	David Caputo
Joseph Rubin	Joseph Afonso

The International Oil Working Group, Inc.
P.O. Box 1014, Cathedral Station
New York, New York, 10025 USA
212 678-1028 & 413 367-9774

Amherst, Massachusetts   February 1989

ISBN # 0-924120-01-0

...USION REPAIRMEN, STUDENTS, SOCIAL WORKERS, COMPUTER PROGRAMMERS, TEACHERS, ENGINEERS, PROSTITUTES, TAXI DRIVERS, OLD, YOUNG
...ALE, MALE, GAY, STRAIGHT, ASIAN, WHITE, BLACK, LATINO, NATIVE AMERICAN, JEWISH, ATHEIST. WE SEE THROUGH THE NARROW TUNNEL
...OUR OWN SEX, RACE, BELIEFS, AND EMPLOYMENT, AND STAY WITHIN A SMALL CIRCLE OF CO-WORKERS AND FRIENDS. UNTIL WE
...AK OUT OF THIS SMALL CIRCLE, LOCAL AND INTERNATIONAL EVENTS ARE UNRELATED TO US OR TO EACH OTHER. DO WE SEE ANY CONNECTIONS
...EEN THEM? AS WE UNLOCK OURSELVES FROM OUR HABITUAL POINT OF VIEW WE SEE COMMON CAUSES AND PATTERNS RECURRING.
...WEREN'T TRAINED TO THINK THIS WAY......WHY? WHO PROFIT WHEN WE ARE ALIENATED FROM EACH OTHER, BLIND TO THE
...UAL SOLUTIONS TO OUR COMMON PROBLEMS? WHO PROFITS WHEN INDUSTRY IS DEREGULATED AND POLLUTION TOLERATED?
...PROFITS WHEN TOXIC CHEMICALS ARE USED TO "WIN" A WAR QUICKLY AND CHEAPLY? WHO PROFITS WHEN THE FERTILE
...OF 3rd WORLD COUNTRIES IS WASTED ON THE "CASH CROPS" OF SUGAR, TOBACCO, AND COFFEE?
...O OWNS THIS MACHINE?

Dedicated to all people who defend cultural democracy

Acknowledgements

We thank Jim Murray, publisher of *Cultural Correspondence*, for his hospitality and help in desktop publishing this book. We are grateful to the people outside of our class for their contributions to us and to this book. We thank Sara Lennox, Director of the Social Thought and Political Economy Program at the University of Massachusetts, for her inspiration. We thank Dan Clawson, John Cole, Vivian Sandlund, Eqbal Ahmad and all the Social Thought and Political Economy professors for their teaching. Helen Johnson and Cynthia Kaufman, STPEC staff, were generous in making available to us the resources of the STPEC office.

We thank Bruce Wilcox, Barbara Wereden, Dede Heath and Risa Mednick of the University of Massachusetts Press for support. We are grateful for the advice of Leo St.Dennis, Elizabeth Callahan and the staff of UMASS Duplicating at Whitmore. Thanks are also due to Seth Tobocman and friends at *World War 3*, Yvonne of Yvonne's Caribbeana Restaurant, David Watson and the staff of the UMASS Craft Center, Arnold Baker, Pedro Pereira and the staff of the *Amherst Bulletin* and *Hampshire Daily Gazette*, Marcia Wright, Jason Talerman and R. Bonanno of the *Collegian*, Deb Donnaly, Christopher Golosh, Ilsa Svensen, Rodrick Thurton, Ralph Reed, John Bracey, Lee Edwards, Calvin Hernton, Margaret Holt, the entire staff of Food For Thought Books; Rey Bin, Fred Contant, Ken Bureau and Carolee Heon of Kinkos; and all the people who encouraged us by their positive reception of our first book *Voices of the Twentieth Century: Our Foremothers Speak.*

We appreciate the contributions of Doris Peterson and the staff of the University of Massachusetts Computer Center. Members of the Social Thought and Political Economy junior seminar deeply appreciate the extra hours which Seminar participants, Leigh Brownhill, Terisa Turner, Amy Pearson, Laura Belanger, John Hanson, Joe Afonso, Timothy Belknap and Matthew Collins, devoted to keeping this project on the peoples' track. Kitty Axelson, editor of the *Valley Advocate* encouraged us at every stage. Jim Murray and Timothy Belknap shared, in a sustained way, their computer literacy with us. There is a large group of people linked to those we've mentioned here; secretaries, lovers, family members, cooks, drivers, housemates, friends, and connections. Thank you for sustaining our capacity to make this book.

We are finally very grateful to our professor, Terisa Turner, for introducing us to C. L. R. James, and for helping us to incorporate his method and spirit into our lives; and, we hope—through this book—into yours.

C.L.R. James

Every American citizen, ignorant of so many things that his European counterpart knows, is conscious of himself as a distinct personality, in his own opinion and the opinion of his fellows, as entitled to special consideration of his ideas, his feelings, his likes and dislikes as the most aristocratic heroine of a European novel. And at the same time he is consumed by the need of intimate communion with his fellows. This is the crisis of the modern world and because of the material conditions and the history of the United States that crisis is here, in every personality, in every social institution, permeating every aspect and every phase of life. I watch it every hour of the day, I have spent countless hours studying American history and American literature, relating the present to the past, estimating the American future. I am profoundly conscious of the deficiencies of American civilization. But they are as nothing to the fact that America is unburdened by the weight of the past which hangs so heavily on Europe, that as a result there is here not culture but a need for human relations of a size and scope which will in the end triumph over all deficiencies.

C.L.R. James
Mariners, Renegades, and Castaways:
The Story of Herman Melville and the World We Live In
(1952)

Our Seminar, November 1988

Upper left to lower right: Jose Afonso,
David Heggestad, Timothy Belknap, Janine
Cardello, Amy Pearson, Ben Bennett, Leigh
Brownhill, Matt Collins, Melissa Hatrak

don't approve of what you did to your own flesh and blood"
-What's the Matter Here?

These strong words inspire those who are toppling the system. These singers appeal to different audiences and voice different concerns. Tracy Chapman digs the deepest, speaking to those affected the most harshly, universally. She offers understanding, validation, spirit and style. She is a part of the revolution that is making the world a place where women will no longer be the shock absorbers for the hell that their husbands go through during the work day. She is part of the revolution of men who are redirecting hostilities away from their families and toward the true agents of frustration and grief. We are all, hand-in-hand, on the move against those who've kept us down so long. "Some folks call her a runaway, a failure in the race, but she knows where her ticket takes her, she will find her place in the sun". Tracy Chapman.

Other sources of revolutionary music, literature analysis and theater:

Domitilla Chungara's *Let Me Speak!*; Rigoberta Menchu's autobiography, *I, Rigoberta Menchu*; *Sweet Honey in the Rock*; *Cassleberry and Dupree*; *Sisteran*, from Jamaica, *the Visisivwe Players* from South Africa; *Ntozake Shange,* writer; Calvin Hernton's book, *The Sexual Mountain and Black Women Writers.* Check it out!

Palestinian women with their children on the West Bank show their support for Israel's Peace Now movement. Paul Tick

C.L.R. James in his home in Brixton, London

C.L.R. JAMES REFLECTS ON AMERICA

C.L.R. James, edited by Jim Murray

The following is the transcript of a 30 minute television show produced by Penumbra Productions, directed by H.O. Nazareth, first shown on Channel Four in Britain on July 4, 1983. It launched a series called "The Best of C.L.R. James" which included talks on cricket, the Caribbean, Shakespeare, Solidarity, and Africa. The questions at the end came from members of the small live audience at the American University in London.

Introduction (Female voiceover)

C.L.R. James, sportsman, political activist, and social visionary, has written classics in history, philosophy, politics, sport, and the arts. Born in 1901 in Trinidad, he has lived in Britain, the United States, and the Caribbean. He has also visited Africa, often as confidant and advisor to progressive political leaders there. E.P. Thompson said of him, "What an extraordinary man C.L.R. is. Everything he has said or done has had the mark of originality, of his own flexible, sensitive and cultured intelligence. He has always conveyed not a rigid doctrine but a delight and curiosity in all the manifestations of life." C.L.R. James is probably the best know West Indian alive.

In 1938 he left Britain for the United States and participated in organizing Black and white tenant farmers in the deep South and workers in Detroit. In 1952 he was expelled from the United States. While in prison awaiting deportation, he wrote *Mariners, Renegades, and Castaways,* a book on the novels of Herman Melville. In the late '50s he co-authored *Facing Reality,* which has had a tremendous impact on Black and white activists in America. James has since taught at several universities, mostly as a professor of humanities in Washington, D.C.

C.L.R. James:

It is a tremendous problem to speak in a half hour about such an enormous civilization as the United States, playing such a tremendous role in the world in which we live. Let us begin with the United States as it is in the world of today. I can compare it to Russia, and I don't know what is your opinion, but I am absolutely bewildered by both of them. Today we have one enormously powerful country preparing to destroy the other country, because it says, "That country is preparing to destroy us," and both of them are only held back -- not by any moral, not by any political, not by any social considerations -- but because their enemy and they themselves have weapons which they call "deterrents." So that we live in a world that does not move to mutual destruction because of a material deterrent. That is the complete degradation of a world that lives by — at least pretends or claims to live by — manners and means and morals.

I look at the world today, at the United States and Russia, and I do not know where they are going. I know that both of them together are an obstacle to any kind of civilization and civilized life. This is my view. I state it quite plainly, because it governs everything that I have to say.

Now the second point. I want to begin from 1929. Today the United State people and their leaders are saying, "We must go back to Coolidge." Coolidge was the man who led the country into its tremendous crisis. It happened to Hoover, but it was Coolidge and his government that for eight years led the United States into that catastrophe. It was not only a catastrophe of the United States, it was a catastrophe of the whole world — the economic breakdown of the capitalist system from which, it is my opinion, it has never recovered. Up till 1929 the United States was governed in the minds of people and by practical means by something that they call "free enterprise." Free enterprise was the capitalist system: did what it could, did what it liked.

But after the crisis, tremendous changes took place in the United States. President Roosevelt said in so many words, "You capitalists will not be allowed to do as you like in the future. The government is going to take charge." And the government took charge, and from 1932 to the present day, we saw in the United States what too many people do not understand: a steady growth of the executive. And free enterprise -- well, a man can start a little factory, and another man can dig a piece of land, but there is no free enterprise. Little by little these huge organizations have grown, but the government is what decides. When there is a problem of wages, it is the government that decides. When there is unemployment, people look to the government. When Japan is sending too many motorcars into the United States, it is the government that decides what is to be done.

The executive has extraordinary power in the United States. Far more than anybody else, it is the executive that is decisive. When the president is voted in, he becomes the executive, he clears out a lot of people, and he puts his own people in. When Carter came in, he brought in a lot of undistinguished, incompetent people from Georgia, and he stuck them there; they made a complete mess of it and had to go. But we find that he had a *right* to do that. The executive is the government of the United States; in the elections the people vote for the executive, and between 1932 and the present, the United States has not been able to work out anything like a stable government.

There was Roosevelt, who formed a body of people who were able to put him back in office for four terms. He brought the Blacks away from the Republican Party, he built the Tennessee Valley Authority, and Roosevelt stayed President until he died because he had a mass of the population behind him. When he died, Truman came in. Nobody expected Truman to be anything but a stand-by president; he contributed nothing except to send bombs to Japan. That was Truman. After Truman we brought in Eisenhower, who did nothing. Adenauer in Germany was doing nothing except to patch it up. Macmillan in England was doing nothing. It seemed that the world was a bit tired after all the exertion, and they drifted along and did nothing in particular.

When Eisenhower was thrown out, Nixon came in, but Kennedy defeated him, and Kennedy defeated him by about 100,000 votes. But Kennedy was shot. Johnson followed, and he won by a large majority, but he got himself tangled up in the Vietnam war and he had to leave, and Nixon came back. We know what happened to Nixon. He had to go—he, his vice president, his attorney general, his head man in internal affairs, his head man in external affairs. They not only went out, they went into jail. And after Nixon came Carter, and Carter was a one-session president.

So I want you to take note that from the time Roosevelt built his organization to the present time when they have Reagan, the   U.S.

C.L.R. James in his home in Brixton, London

government, which is the executive, has not been able to win over any section of the population to acquire that authority which enables you to govern. That is U.S. history since the Depression. In other words, up to the present day, there has been nothing but disorder, confusion, and inability to form anything which can form the basis for any steady development of the American economy. It is impossible to come to any decisions as to where the economy is going and what is to be done to bring it into some sort of order. It is impossible to go to any social group that will give a direction to the life and the economy and the society of the country.

I want you to understand: that country does not know where it is going. I don't believe that any foreign minister has made so many blunders and created such confusion as Mr. Alexander Haig. People are always having to come to his support, because he says one thing and does one thing, and then he does something else and says something else and does not know where he is going. The president has to come to his support and say, "We are all very good friends. We are all very happy going along." But that's why it's impossible. That is the state of the country both politically and economically.

I now have to talk about the Black people in the United States. They are one of the most dynamic elements in the development of United States society. What is the greatest event in the history of the United States? It is the Civil War, by which the feudal elements in the South were finished. That Civil War was prepared by, among other people, the Blacks, who kept on running away from the estates in the South into the North, and more than that, by the activity of the abolitionist movement, which was one of the greatest political events in the United States between 1830 and 1860.

When we look at the people who were subscribing to the papers, we find that the majority of these were Black people. They kept up a constant agitation, so that the South was never at peace, and many liberal-minded people in the North could not turn their minds away from the fact that Blacks in the North who were not slaves could not get jobs, for instance. They were spending their time in agitation about slavery, while the slaves kept up the underground railroad and kept the country in a state of continuous disorder. That agitation brought on the Civil War.

In regard to the Civil War itself I can only paraphrase Abraham Lincoln: "If the Blacks who are fighting with us and working with us were to leave us, in three weeks the South would have won the war. You complain that I am fighting a war for the abolition of slavery. I am not doing that. I am fighting a war for the unity of the country. But if the Blacks were to leave us -- those who are fighting in the war, 200,000 of them -- we would lose the war in three weeks." People don't seem to know that, and I can't understand it.

Abraham Lincoln at his Second Inaugural made one of the greatest speeches that I have ever heard from any bourgeois politician. He had won the election; it wasn't a speech made for the sake of winning some votes. He said, "If every drop of wealth created by the bondsmen — 250 years of unrequited labor — were to be destroyed, and every drop of blood given by the whip was to be repaid by one drawn with the sword, still shall it be said that the judgments of the Lord set forth 3000 years ago are true and righteous altogether." That's the Second Inaugural Address. That's a tremendous speech, but nobody seems to know it. He said, "I don't care what they did; I'm going to put that right. We are going to repay them for what was done and make everything as it should be, taking into consideration the sufferings they have had for 250 years." And a little afterwards he was shot. That's why he was shot. People talk about "government of the people, by the people" -- that is not the speech that matters. The one that matters is the Second Inaugural. That is Lincoln, and white Americans know that. White Americans know that.

Mr. Ramsey Clark, who was Johnson's Attorney General, once wrote in an article I read, "There are five million students giving us a lot of trouble." Those were the days when the students were wrecking the universities or other institutions. "We have about thirty million Blacks," he said, "and if the Blacks and the students were to join together, the American government would be in a great difficulty."

Martin Luther King was a Doctor of Divinity and he taught many educated Black people that you not only wrote letters to your congressman and held meetings, but you took to the streets. So many of them who had remained in their houses all the time took to the streets behind Martin Luther King. And then King began to see that the Vietnam war was a violation of the American Constitution and of the

American people. And they faced the possibility that King, who had all the Blacks behind him, would know of the students, who were against the war, and that would throw the government into complete disorder and disarray. And that is why they shot Martin Luther King.

Now I am going to read for you a passage from a book by Theodore White, *Breach of Faith: The Fall of Richard Nixon*. This is not about the Blacks who in the '60s came into the streets; this is about the white students. When Nixon and Kissinger sent the army into Cambodia, about a quarter of a million, three to four hundred thousand people marched in Washington to let Nixon know: "We disapprove of this; we don't think that you are doing right."

Listen to this: "Whether or not Richard Nixon came close to a nervous breakdown in the events of May 1970 is debated seriously by his aides." Americans like to think of nervous breakdown and single individuals. They don't like to think about political terms, that's too dangerous. Nixon had spoken that evening on television (I think he called the students "bums"). Then he tried to fall asleep but sleep eluded him. "At 10:35 that evening, he began to reach out by telephone: to Rose Mary Woods, his secretary; to his daughter Tricia; to Secretary of State William Rogers; two minutes later to Henry Kissinger (10:37); to Bob Haldeman a minute later (10:38); to Mrs. Nixon a minute thereafter (10:39); to Dr. Norman Vincent Peale (10:50) — and then, racking up thirty-eight more calls in three hours, he ran on: Transportation Secretary Volpe, Congressman Fountain, Hobart Lewis, William Safire, Secretary Shultz, Secretary Laird, Henry Kissinger again, Billy Graham, John Ehrlichman, Bob Haldeman (a second time), Secretary Hickel, Rose Mary Woods (second), Bebe Rebozo, Pat Moynihan, Congressman Monaghan, Haldeman (third), Cliff Miller, Rose Woods (third). It was now past midnight and the calls went on: Haldeman again at 12:18, Haldeman again at 12:20, Kissinger again at 12:24, and Alexis Johnson, Kissinger, Haldeman, Ziegler, Buchanan, Kissinger, Nelson Rockefeller (at two minutes of one in the morning), Herb Klein, newscaster Nancy Dickerson, Ziegler, newswoman Helen Thomas, Bebe Rebozo again, John Mitchell, Governor Thomas Dewey, Bob Haldeman again, Rose Woods again, Kissinger again at five minutes of two in the morning. Then came a pause. At 3:24 he began telephoning again — to Paul Keyes, to Kissinger (3:38 a.m.), to Ron Ziegler, to Helen Thomas."

The students had taken over Washington, and that was Nixon's reply. He had no defense against them. That is the United States. Page 172. I recommend it to you.

I will leave you for the last with what happened in the '60s. For a hundred years and more, southern white people had persecuted, maltreated, and generally kicked around the Black people, and the Black students went down there and sat down in the restaurants and said, "I want a cup of coffee." They said, "We don't serve Blacks." They said, "We'll stay here until you do." They burnt the fingers of the hands of the young men with cigarettes. They set dogs after them. Do you remember that? They did everything. And the Blacks sat through it. And finally they gave in. They had to give in, because the Blacks were determined. But the Blacks started something, after which the students and a whole lot of people joined.

Blacks are the ones who began the activity which the rest of the United States has followed. I want you to remember that the United States is not what many people think it is. It is a country in which the great forces which make up that country are in movement, and good-ness knows what the results of that movement will be. I know what I hope they will be. But that they are in movement, I want you to know. There is taking place in the United States some serious disorder from below, and it is shooting up with these odd spectacles. And they imply that sooner or later all that is moving below is going to move with greater force.

Thank you very much.

QUESTIONS

Q: C.L.R., do you think there is any kind of hope for the United States? Because you paint a very dim and dark picture for, let's say, a revival of good old-fashioned Roosevelt New Deal coalition politics.

A: No, I see no opportunity of the United States going back to the old free enterprise days. The Black people are not going to take it anymore. In addition, they have a new set of people, the Chicanos, who are following what the Blacks have done and what the Blacks have gained, and they are not taking it any more. If Mr. Reagan has a policy, it is to go back to Coolidge. Believe me, I am astonished at how anybody could want to go back to Coolidge. It is beyond me to go back to Coolidge, because Coolidge led straight into the Depression. In the United States, the feeling is that we are in a hell of a mess and we don't know which way to come out of it.

Q: Yes, but what kind of mess is it? From abroad it's a very high standard of living; they have a lot of pleasurable activities. What is this mess?

A: Because people do not live according to a standard of living. They live according to their conception of the society where they are, what is taking place, where their children are going to be developed and educated. They must have some sense of certainty and of a general direction. That is what America today is losing day after day.

Q: Away from the White House, away from the big Democratic and Republican parties, do you see anybody inside the United States making a sensible, progressive politics out of what you call a mess?

A: I saw the other day some quarter of a million people calling themselves Solidarity meet in Washington for a demonstration against the Reagan government. Do you remember that? Everybody was astonished. What had happened to the United States working class that they called themselves Solidarity like the Polish working class? In the past the Blacks have spoken in this respect. The Chicanos have spoken, the women have spoken, the students have spoken. And the labor movement, it seems today, has decided that it too is going to speak.

Q: I believe that Washington, D.C. is where you were teaching for many years. I wonder if you could tell us some of the things that your Black students said about their aspirations in American society.

A: I have found among the boys of seventeen, eighteen, twenty-one that they realize they themselves cannot carry on some individual kind of struggle. But they are meeting together in groups and reading and studying hard. They are waiting for something, but they are determined that what is going on will not continue. In fact, some of them have told me, "We may not be able to change the society and create what you all call a socialist society. But what has gone on for 100 years will not continue. And we today are numerous enough and patient enough to bring this society down if it does not make things right." But they are not in a hurry. They are waiting to see.

Q: During the election of 1980, Arthur Schlesinger, writing in the *Wall Street Journal*, indicated that because of the myths involved in the economic policies of both candidates -- President Carter and candidate Reagan -- he anticipated that the masses of the poor would take their destinies into their own hands.

A: He is very rash. I can never dare to say when the people will take their destinies into their own hands. That is something that only the people know, and they don't know until the time comes when they do it. But the United States people on the whole are very much aware of the uncertainty in the population. That is a fact. That is what I have been trying to tell you. And the ruling class in the United States and some of the middle classes are very much aware of the fact that the people take their destiny into their own hands. But when that will be, I don't know.

This document is published by the C.L.R. James Institute. All rights reserved by C.L.R. James and Penumbra Productions. Production assistance: Avis Lang. The Institute invites comments from all readers, which will then become a part of the C.L.R. James Archive. Address all correspondence to the Institute's Director, Jim Murray, 505 West End Avenue, N.Y. N.Y 10024

Women and Recession in Petroleum Exporting Societies: the Case of Trinidad and Tobago

Donna Coombs, edited by Melissa Hatrak

Editorial note: Donna Coombs, who is an educator and a researcher for the Oilfields Workers Trade Union of Trinidad, delivered this lecture at Smith College in Northampton, Massachusetts on April 20th, 1988. Her lecture was tape recorded. I have transcribed the tape. Terisa Turner and I have inserted minor changes in the text for the purposes of clarity. I've also included excerpts from the question and answer period which followed the lecture. As of February 1989, when we printed this book, Donna Coombs had not yet proofread the following text.

Donna Coombs: Good evening, I would like to thank the students and faculty, particularly Terisa Turner, for giving me this opportunity to interact with you, to share some experiences and to share some ideas. I've been here and in New York with Terisa since Tuesday night. When your hanging out here with Terisa you have to have a lot of stamina because you run from one end of the city to the other and wherever she's going to take you.

What I'm going to do is give you some information about life in Trinidad, the struggle for power of all the classes, the role that American companies have been playing, and particularly within that context, the expanding role of women in the movement for change.

Oil, Sugar, and Imperialism

Let me give you some background history. Trinidad is an English speaking eastern Caribbean island. It's just seven miles from Venezuela, just hanging on to the tip of the southern archipelago that spans from Bermuda coming right down to Venezuela in South America. We have historically been a British colony that gained its independence in 1962.

Since independence, there have been struggles between the forces in Trinidad and Tobago for the control over our destiny and our resources. We are an oil producing country. Oil has, for the last fifty or sixty years, dominated our economy to the extent that the amount of revenue it has provided for the government let's say between 1973 and 1983, during the period of the oil boom, remains something like sixty-seven billion dollars from revenue, from taxes of corporations and that kind of thing. So you can imagine how much the corporations have made. By corporations, I mean Amoco which was originally based in Indiana, Texaco which is world wide, and Texaco-Trinidad incorporated which sold out its land holdings in 1985, but still has its marine holdings in Trinidad, from which they make about fifty million U.S. dollars per year. So we are a quite lucrative business for the oil companies.

We've had an obscure oil corporation called Tesoro Corporation, some of you may have never heard of it, it's located in San Antonio, Texas. In the sixties there was a movement among the British oil companies to get out (of the country). During that period the government bought British petroleum's holdings in the area. Although we had been producing oil commercially since 1907, the government didn't have the confidence that we the nationals, were capable of running the industry. So they went hunting for a partner, and they found this little company in San Antonio named Tesoro, which had one little outlet, and they brought them down. British Petroleum charged forty-four million for their holdings, we were to pay twenty-two million U.S. dollars for our half of the holdings, but Tesoro came down with only fifty thousand U.S. dollars for their half. So we paid twenty two million and then we sold the other half for fifty thousand dollars, of which they paid ten thousand dollars in cash, and forty thousand dollars worth of our oil, oil which was to be produced in the future, so in the end we ourselves paid for their half.

In the third world countries, that's the kind of transactions you find in the interest of the multinational company or the foreign company. They have a vested interest in coming to third world countries because of the profits they will get, and many of our government officials, if they are in charge, also have a vested interest in lining their pockets, this being just a front for them to be corrupt officials. They can use Tesoro to funnel money to some foreign bank account. That's how they treat us! So very often you find that our resources are not being used in our interest to benefit our people, and it is very important for you to know that.

Wages are kept low, and resources are abused because somehow it seems to benefit the companies here in the U.S., somehow when the profits are expatriated to here, we don't benefit from that, but we provide the natural resources. So very often you find our natural resources, for instance our refined oil, finds its way back to be used to heat homes in the U.S. For many decades that's the role we've played with Texaco. In Haiti they make baseballs. In fact the largest baseball factories are in Haiti and no one plays baseball there. It's totally for export. This is the kind of role we play and this is important for you to understand.

So here we are in Trinidad, an oil producing country, which, yes, is producing revenue for government coffers, but more of it is coming back out by way of profits. So Tesoro came down in '69, after they paid ten thousand in cash for their fifty percent of that operation and they left in '86, and before they left, they demanded from the government 297 million dollars U.S. for the same half that we gave them in 1969. It has been so lucrative for them, that they bragged about it for years. They were able to buy a refinery in Puerto Rico and expand their operations in other countries because of the wealth or the profits which they generated in Trinidad and Tobago. It's well documented in sources; I'm sure you can find it in your library.

So basically we are an oil producing country. Oil has replaced sugar. Sugar used to be the major commodity at the turn of the century but there was a decline in the demand for cane sugar as it was replaced by beet sugar, so it is no longer a lucrative business. And let's face it, we have been producing sugar for Britain for centuries. We propped up the British treasury for centuries and allowed them to expand their operations and conquer so many colonies and people. We were tired of producing sugar and had developed a kind of hatred for the sugar plantation because it was synonymous with slavery. So when slavery was abolished people just didn't want to see sugar any more although we're still involved in sugar production because there are all these vast hectares of acres of land which have been involved in sugar cane production for so many centuries.

There is now a struggle to try to diversify the agriculture to meet our domestic needs. About 90% of our sugar is produced to meet export demands. We are so export oriented that we've had to import most of what we consume because there is no indigenous productive base for agricultural commodities. We are importers of our food and exporters of our oil. The things we need, the clothes we need, and the food we need, we import, that's how the economy is presently structured.

The Expanding Role of Women

Recently, because of the oil boom in the 70's and early 80's and the revenue the government was able to accrue from state owned companies and the multinationals, there was a lot of rapid expansion in industry in a lot of light manufacturing, heavy manufacturing, and assembly plants of all sorts, so that thousands of women were able to come into productive labor for the first time. A lot of house workers were now being paid wages for the labor they were expending to produce things like televisions, radios, garments, and edible oils. People got into all different kinds of deals or production, some of them locally owned.

So it gave rise to a whole new grouping, a whole new class of local capitalists and conglomerates rose up or entrenched themselves in this period, because of the profits now available or the profits being generated locally through banks or insurance companies and that kind of thing. So that for the first time what we were finding in our society is that women who were houseworkers before, like our mothers who never had a proper education, and slaved all day to cloth us, send us off to school to give us a proper education, alot of them were able to join us in the ranks of the working force.

You find a lot of single parents at home. Women before had to try to meet the man wherever he was working and beg him for a few dollars on Friday evenings if he was paid weekly. That's how you would get some sustenance for the children because the laws are very weak when it comes to the protection of the family or of the woman who must bare this burden by herself. We women who were forced to do that in order to obtain a few dollars from the fathers of our children now were working for the first time so we had economic independence. That is what the oil boom meant for many women. We no longer had to subject ourselves to this kind of abuse then,where there was an option to give to you or he didn't, or his friends at work would say he didn't come today, or you would have to find out where he was living, or that kind of devious means to obtain some support which should really be seen as his responsibility.

So now you find that women are working and women are getting involved actively in the struggle to defend their own rights as workers,and your finding that more women are obtaining a higher level of education. So alongside women as workers in production, in manufacturing, and so on, a class of women professionals, women teachers, lawyers, doctors, and so on, was mushrooming as a vehicle in this society. However one area where the struggle for equality of employment was never realized was in heavy industry. There are absolutely no women working in oil, in production or refining. There are no women in electricity, generation or distribution. There are no women in steel, and there are no women in these strategic areas which is the hub of how this society turns, with electricity and oil and heavy commodities and steel.

There are no women as if by some unwritten law. This has never been a struggle. We have not matured to that level were we can demand that an employer hire five percent, or however many women in oil production and steel. In fact, what has happened right now is that they've decided to close down the steel plants because they are unproductive and very expensive for us to maintain. It has cost us something like five billion dollars over the last ten years to just keep it open and keep it employed. We have been fined for dumping here on the U.S. market because they were selling below the market price, and all that kind of thing, so there are international marketing politics involved in that.

But generally, in the government owned steel plant they have never hired a woman except in the traditional areas of office workers and the cafeteria and maybe the new clinic and that kind of thing. The same occurs in the electrical industry, again we are restricted to the traditional jobs. These are the areas where even in the ranks of the fight back movement, a struggle has not been waged. Neither has it been waged for daycare centers attached to factories. Many of the proposals we (in the oil union) have written for various companies' workers who we represent have requested that daycare center facilities, or some fringe benefit be provided to allow single parents in particular, and women in general access to such facilities. But it has not been a campaign as yet where we can say we have won this battle or maybe gained in this area. This is still a battle to be fought.

We Learn Through The Culture

The battles we have been fighting have been in the areas of sexual harassment. Related to this issue is how we're affected in our culture by the Calypsonian. Calypso and steel band are two very indigenous parts of our culture. The steel drum is the only musical instrument to be created in the twentieth century. Its a very interesting instrument. The Calypso or the Calypsonian is the mouthpiece. Just like country and western music has a particular meaning and message to the American people; similarly for us the Calypso and the Calypsonian is the barometer of change which is coming down the road. The Calypsonian sings about the society, about the struggles, about the positions of solidarity we take on Nicaragua, and we were singing about Noriega before the U.S. engaged in the present campaign to isolate Panama last year.

Calypso is about Panama because what was happening before was when our corrupt officials ran away with our money they were going to Panama, so in fact this year the most popular Calypso, "I'm going to Panama, I've got to go to Panama Mama", so the people were asking what is this about Panama, "what is this they have over there", something about money, "they're going by tens of thousands", that's about the money they're taking, so we learn through the culture. This is a place were those with Swiss bank accounts or tourists stash away illegal money obtained through hard drugs and what have you. Panama has been a back door depository for spiriting away some of the hard earned money which belongs to the people of Trinidad and Tobago.

So the Calypsonian sings about these issues, about South Africa, how many more must die before South Africa is free, we sing about our struggles and about the things which concern us most, and for years they have sung about women in the most sexist fashion. They have always described us as sexual objects in the past, "Jean and Dina,

Rosita, and Clementina," (Donna Coombs is singing) these are prostitutes "round the corner posing, bet your life there's something they're
selling", now they're selling their flesh, and the Calypsonian is singing
about that, as if all women in Trinidad were engaged in that trade. Well
they stopped now because we're demanding more respect. There is a
competition we have every year during the Calypso season. In the finals
of the Calypso competition, the judges who had auditioned, who hear
how they present the songs and how they come over the lyrics and the
melody, starting from four hundred being auditioned in the Calypso
arenas where they performed during this year, work it down to twenty-four semi-finalists, and eight for the finals, so to reach in the top
eight, eight out of 400, is a big deal.

I was telling Terisa just yesterday that eight of the twenty-four
semi-finalists in the Calypso Competition for 1988 were women. For
the first time in our history this year, we had two women reach the finals.
And the songs were very, very strong this year about the women's
movement. One woman is singing "woman is boss," another woman is
singing, "pop for pop, if he pop me I'm popping him back", and women
are looking at women from a progressive and an independent
standpoint, and they are saying we aren't taking any more stuff, we've
taken enough blows, we've taken enough abuse, and we've just had
enough of that. Another woman is singing about a woman coming in
from the cold, "rise up, rise up and make your mark", and another
woman is singing how do you describe a beautiful woman, is it by her
fine cheekbone or her pencilled eyebrows, or properly shaped lips or
her equal teeth or what have you, or is it by how much she protects her
family, or how much she slaves to insure that her children are clothed,
and these other values which we learned to disregard. That's what
they're singing about: how do we value a woman? Is it how she looks
in the skimpiest of bathing suits which is how we're taught to evaluate
ourselves, is it how much her breasts still are firm, you do not look at
how many children she has nursed with those same breasts. That's what
the Calypsonians are singing about, women are singing about themselves, and so they're singing that we should have more self respect and
we should stand up for what is rightfully ours, which is full equality in
this society and that's a new trend for us.

In fact one of our older Calypsonians who has sung a lot in the
United States is called Sparrow. He has been singing since 1956. Like

other immigrants who came in the twenties and thirties Sparrow came from Grenada. Some of you may have heard about the island of Grenada. Sparrow came to Trinidad in search of employment in the oil industry because, just like there is migration to the U.S. there is migration among the Caribbean islands. Trinidad being an oil based economy has attracted people from the other English speaking islands to work in the oil industries. We have large communities of people from Saint Vincent's called Vincentians, or people from Dominica called Dominicans, or people from Grenada which is just 90 miles from us called Grenadians, and Sparrow is one of them. He has traditionally been an advocate of progressive views in Calypso.

This year he got an honorary doctorate from the university for his contribution to Calypso over the last thirty years, and also this year he's singing about this woman who thought Sparrow was a medical doctor so she came to him for treatment, and she's saying that she wants something there, some injection there, something up somewhere, something he raised up there, somewhere he went at her body, and people just totally ridiculed him. They were saying, we have passed that stage Sparrow, as much we value the contribution you made to Calypso we don't want that stuff any more. There were letters in the press about how disappointed people felt about how he took his doctorate and what he did with it, because for the first time in our history an artist of his level was receiving an honorary document and what's he singing about? He's ridiculing the woman, and people were just 'lambasting' him, as we say at home, for doing that with such an honorary position.

Women Organizing

That's what we are doing now, women are just standing up to be recognized. In our union we are participating in this growing movement which is seeing several women's organizations mushrooming, women are getting together in groups to fight for certain issues. For international women's day this year we had a consultation, and the focus was on the economic measures of the new regime. I've mentioned they had elections in December '86, in which the present government overthrew the old People's National Movement, which had been in power for thirty years. Although their oppositional stance during the campaign was that there was not enough women in leadership roles in government, and that there was not enough recognition of women's contributions, they have since abandoned that position.

They no longer talk about that, they just have a few token appointments in the traditionally not serious areas like community development. Their present policies are in the hands of a man who has always been described as a CIA spokesman in Trinidad and Tobago, who is not involved in any way with elections but who has been given a senior appointment in the government to run all industry, all state enterprises and is second to the Prime Minister who often directs the Prime Minister. His position or his push is for us to set up these export processing zones. In radical politics it's called runaway shop. You may have heard about it studying economics. When a corporation or companies find that the U.S. worker is demanding to much by way of wages or benefits they pack up over night and run to Taiwan, or they run to some third world country.

That's what baseballs are doing in Haiti because Haitians get fourteen dollars a week, and that's fourteen Haitian dollars which is a mere fraction of a U.S. dollar. So it's very lucrative for them to pack up shop and run, so they call it run away shop. You run after cheap labor and favorable government conditions, you get tax free concessions, and they give you the land. We have a ten year pioneer status where you are the only person who can produce a certain commodity in a region of thousands of miles, that kind of thing, very favorable conditions.

From our standpoint standing there looking up, job's are running to third world countries. We are being prepared for areas designated especially for export processing zones, where they can come and set up shop practically unconditionally. They often buy officials in government, trade unions are outlawed, security guards check you in the morning to make sure you don't bring anything or take anything out, and they check all your teeth if they have to, like in South Africa, to make sure that you don't steal anything to compensate for your low wages. You have to ask permission to go out to the bathroom. Very often these are the conditions that you find in export processing zones. The policy of the new government is they are going to settle our employment problems by setting up these export processing zones.

At the International Women's Day celebrations this year the purpose of our consultations was to try to get into what these zones are about, and whether we wanted them in Trinidad and Tobago. They have been tried all over the third world and they have not solved the problems of unemployment. They have dehumanized people, that's what they have done. They have forced very many women to be sterilized because these are the conditions they have imposed on you, that you've got to limit how many pregnancies you can have, without losing you job. In some cases once you get pregnant you are dismissed, or when you sign the application they send you to the doctor to be sterilized. That's how you get your job and that's how your going to keep it, so they know that absence from work wouldn't be a problem because of children or because of pregnancy. It's very inhuman, these export processing zones, or free zones. They have different names, they call it but they're always zones, zones of imposition, zones of U.S. or British companies, or whoever is coming in to your land and using your resources.

They have an empire within your boundaries, within your lands which they call their own, where you are forbidden, and that's how they operate. So our focus right now is to fight against the threats of the impositions of these zones that we don't want, you know. They force unionized workers who have worked for five or six hundred dollars a week, to work for seventy five dollars a week. Very often they impose such high levels of production, the quota that you have to meet, that you could never meet production to make the extra twenty dollar bonus that you need. And very often you find that it costs you more to get to work then what you earn in wages. So it has never been found to be the solution to employment problems in the case in Taiwan or on a permanent basis. It may work for a year or two, until people are just wondering, "What is going on here? Who am I really working for? What am I really getting out of it? I haven't been able to pay the bills I owed from before that." So very often you find that this is an experience which makes you more mature. We have learned throughout the third world from our brothers and sisters, that these zones have not been a solution to unemployment. So that is the kind of thing we're presently involved in.

Grenada

In my union, in my particular department which is educational research, I am responsible for the information which flows through the organization, and I feed it into the archives, and make it available to people in the university. I provide whatever we have, and whatever I can acquire. Information doesn't flow in Trinidad as easily as we would like. For instance, even to get a subscription to a foreign magazine you have to get foreign exchange. They make you wait six months to get fifty-two dollars to buy a subscription to *Business Week*. We have to depend on international sources where we can, to assist us, in order to educate our people so that we can help each other learn about what is good for us and what is bad for us. It's important for us to know what stand your taking here, and what stand we should be taking at home, so we can support each other. It's important for you to know the facts behind what they're doing to us down here so that you can have a voice to speak up here, and so there can be more strength in your voice, whether it's on the issue of Nicaragua, or on the issue of Grenada. Let me digress for a minute on the issue of Grenada.

Grenada was a very explosive situation for us, particularly us in Trinidad and Tobago because we are ninety miles away. It's the first time in my living experience that I've witnessed a U.S. invasion of a country as small as Grenada, which is only 110,000 people. It's very close to us in Trinidad and Tobago. My grandmother's from Tobago, and we have a lot of inter-island exchange. Seventy percent of the oil belt community I grew up in are people born in Grenada, who came as adults to work in the oil fields. So we are very close to Grenada.

There was an experiment going on in Grenada from '79-'83, where people of that third world country were experimenting with change. But there were problems with it, there was a split in the leadership. People who had a vested interest in power, sought to oppose the regime that was popular and democratically organized to suit the environment in which people were living. This popular regime was trying to maintain the administration of the country in a way that would benefit the people of Grenada, while experimenting with new forms of local and central government. There is nothing wrong with experimentation because we are all students of change. That's why we are here at college or university, to learn about law, or about what Nicaragua means to

Central America, or about what New York means to the whole of the United States by way of one state within a collection of states. That is what education is. We do something with the knowledge, we experiment, we go into a lab, whether it is a social lab, a political lab, or a chemical lab and we experiment. So we are experimenting in Grenada with what kind of knew administration we would like to see.

In an ex-colony of the size of Grenada where there is very limited natural resources where people come from a colonial background, we have been taught to be proper. We usually accept that we have to go to universities abroad, that we have to go to England and sound like the Queen which we all do very well. We use knives and forks and we're proper and we look down on those who have not had any equal opportunity like our parents and our grandparents. We try to aspire to those qualities which make us intellectual or middle class or what have you. Then we try to even rise higher. We try to make it sound like getting rich were an equal opportunity for all, which it's not. So that's what we have been trained into, that's what we've been taught as colonial subjects. They lend you their passport till they don't want you to have it any more and then you can't go back to your so called mother country which has been your mother for centuries. You have to go under new conditions. They have and all these restrictions now, because they don't need you any more.

So now this is Grenada. We're in the middle of the Caribbean. It's just under one hundred and ten thousand people, mainly black, with a sprinkling of other nationalities. They try to make a break from the Westminster system, which is what we've inherited, the British system which you broke from in 1776. A round of applause for you. Now that's what we're trying to do. We've inherited this system which doesn't suit our needs. The struggle against it is at different levels at different islands. People are trying to break from this traditional mode of the Westminster method. It's this we must lose. In Grenada they tried that and there were problems with the attempt. There were people aspiring to power and there were people that the masses held up saying,"these are our leaders, these are the ones we want to direct us."

Coard Kills Bishop and the U.S.A. Invades

There was Maurice Bishop and his allies on one side, and there's Bernard Coard and his breed on the other side, and there's a show down. The masses say we want Bishop. So even though he's arrested they free him. And somehow Reagan decides that this is an opportunity to kill the idea of revolution in Grenada once and for all, so he invades. Nobody wanted a U.S. invasion in the Caribbean. We consider it an invasion. There wasn't any invitation.

Later, after they invaded they decided that Regina Childs from Dominica, in exchange for certain grants and funds she was supposed to get through the Caribbean Basin Initiative program, would be the mouthpiece. So they raised the excuse that she called up Reagan and somehow just like that his troops were there in a matter of minutes.

Do you know how long it takes to organize all these people to invade a country with helicopters? In the first instance all the sailors who were going home for the weekend have to be instructed they can't go. They have to go to Grenada instead of going home to their wives and their children. You have to get food. In the event that the invasion takes months you have to prepare organizationally for the whole operation. And Reagan's trying to say in a matter of minutes they left wherever they left, and landed in Grenada with the collaboration of some of our traitors in the Caribbean, like Tom Adams (from Barbados) who is now dead.

We in Trinidad had no part in that. In fact because the government at the time took the stand that it would not be involved in any invasion of any Caribbean island, we were ostracized. The C.I.A. worked night and day to assist in getting our government (the Peoples National Movement) out of power. We wanted them out too, but we did not want the C.I.A. in our elections, which they orchestrated to ensure that the party that was entrenched at the time would lose. They funded the new party to the tune of thousands of dollars. They have all these ways and means hidden, legal and illegal, through which they manipulate us. And so Grenada was an experience for us.

We saw to what lengths the U.S. would go to ensure that the Monroe Doctrine was followed. Whether we liked it or not, we are in the U.S.'s back yard and we will do what Reagan says. It was Grenada yesterday, and it was Nicaragua yesterday and today, and it's Panama today and tomorrow, and maybe one day it will be Trinidad and Tobago. So this is why I thought it would be important for you to understand how we feel.

We will solve our problems in our way just like you will solve yours. We can't invade New York. We can't invade Detroit. We have to depend on the U.S. people to oppose the Botha regime. This is how we depend on our solidarity. We have to depend on you to be our international allies because we need each other. That's the main message I wanted to bring to you today, that everyone has a role to play, everyone has a brain and a mouth, and everyone has to understand. To me it's an obligation to understand the issues which effect your country, your government your politics, and your direction.

It's important for everyone to understand the Jesse Jackson/Dukakis issue. We are following it very closely at home. Whatever happens here effects us. We follow everything that happens here because thousands of our nationals live here and contribute here, just like other countries have nationals here. So it's important to have that exchange and we value that very highly. I was very glad for the opportunity to come up and share some thoughts with you. I have been talking for too long, so I should pause to ask if you have any particular concerns which I haven't addressed.

They Fear An Organized Response

Q: If Trinidad and Tobago is invaded, are inter-national solidarity and public relations their main weapon in surviving the invasion?

DC: Well it is and it is more than that.It is whatever solidarity, or other means, that will be required at the time to enable us to continue living and solving our problems internally without outside interference. But once you have foreign companies there, the class struggle continues you see. The corporations purpose in being there is to export whatever commodities or profits they can accrue from their investments. Our interest in being there is to live, and to save our natural resources. So we are already on a confrontation course. It may become more open at some point. We have run out many companies. They just

72

take off like thieves in the night, they 'run away shop' from down there too, once the workers start rebelling and say, "it's about time you got toilets in there, I'm tired of peeing in the corner," or that kind of thing, whatever the issue is. You see, these companies spend as little as possible, in order to make sure most of the money or revenue is in the form of profits. And the profit margin widens constantly. In fact Amoco is called a spit-and-rubber-band company. Because as wealthy as they are, and as big and powerful as they are, they use the cheapest means in order to patch up leaky pipes and that kind of thing.

People get killed all the time and you don't even know about it, because oil workers are offshore. Unless a worker who witnesses an accident goes to the press, no one knows how many cranes knock off how many heads, or how many people fall in the sea. You just know that one of your menfolk hasn't come home, and then you find out that he died in some accident on the job. They try to keep this sort of thing out of the press so we rely on the workers a lot to inform us about what's going on at Amoco. Their corporate practices are very bad, because they have so much control in the government they don't need to respect your sovereignty and to treat you like human beings.

Our union at the request of the workers of Amoco have applied for recognition. That's the only thing they fear, they fear an organized response.

Talking About A Revolution

The movement of the people of Trinidad and Tobago is about trying to have the people control their own resources. We have the skills, we have the technological development. We have enough of the expertise and the exposure to develop domestic industries that we can control. We can develop export relations with other societies that suit our mutual conditions. It doesn't have to be because we are aligned this way or that way. ... It's about time that we get the kind of confidence that we never have had before. We have had someone else decide for us. You see, it was British before and now it's American. It was British Petroleum before and now it's Amoco, or it's Canadian Imperial Bank of Commerce, or Citibank, it's all of those foreign interests. Where are we in all that? What role do we play? Right now that's the role of the people? It's about time there was another revolution, that there is

73

another revolution which awakens the spirit of nationalism and patriotism we are yearning for.

We are tired of the video rock concerts every Saturday night. We don't see enough of our own culture on our own television. We see our carnival for two weeks in February. The rest of the year we could tell you anything about *The Young and the Restless*, anything you want to know about *Dynasty*, anything you want to know about Hunter. We get all of them, and the television is the broadest medium of communication at home. It's all over the society, that kind of domination, and we're trying to deal with it, to shake it off.

There is a movement now to develop more local programming, which the government is fighting. But organizations of independent media are getting together to form a lobby. The lobby is trying to force the government to release the second television station at home so that locals can develop our skills in television production. Then we could stop depending on imported packages and all the garbage we're forced to watch. When the U.S. television transmission is finished the Trinidad station just switches off. It's cheaper than paying locals to just import these planned packages.

So you get *The Young and the Restless* for three hours on a Saturday evening and then you get *Dynasty* for the next three hours. You can miss it all week and sit for three hours and consume all of it in one go. It's a crime that you often have to fight your own family because people get really hooked into that. They don't see how they are taught to imitate people they will never be. It's in the culture, it's in the politics, it's in the economics, and it's a terrible struggle, but we're putting up a hell of a fight.

Taking to the Streets

Q: How do people control political power? How often do you get to elect or vote for the people in the political structure who are supposedly representing you the mass of people?

DC: O.K., the question is how do we the mass of people select our leadership, or how often do we get a vote or chose the government in power. We have the Westminster system which is British. We have a

74

parliament with six elected seats which are contested every five years. They have a maximum of five years in power, unless they extend themselves through some state of emergency and postpone elections. There are contending parties and you are requested to vote for whichever party you chose. Now what you find since the '66 elections, is that the percentage of voter turnout has been just over 50%, because the people don't see that the elections have resolved unemployment, or the immediate issues facing us.

There has been a hard-core of support behind the party which has been in power since 1956, the Peoples National Movement. However there was a dramatic swing in the last election of 1986 away from the Peoples National Movement and to a new alliance which is composed of the extreme right, some central forces, and some left of center organizations called the United Labor Front. These allied together in order to create the National Alliance for Reconstruction which is the party in power now. This party campaigned on a lot of liberal issues, and had liberal positions on a lot of issues, and had a very progressive manifesto. But the party has since disillusioned the masses tremendously and has done more damage than was done the thirty years before.

They are very unpopular. The mood at home is that in a few months we can expect some kind of revolt because we just can't take anymore. Public servants have had no wage increase since 1983, not the police, not the army. The people have been just hanging on. Inflation has been going out of control. ... Senior governmental ministers have been dismissed in the last couple of months. The deputy prime minister and some other high ministers have been dismissed, they are having their own shakeup, and they are disillusioned people. They are heading for another storm in the coming months. So at some point you'll being reading that masses in Trinidad and Tobago are revolting again. It's not going to be in the polls this time. They are going to be taking to the streets. There are already signs of that taking place. There are quite a few healthy signs that people are dissatisfied with how they are living.

The government cut twenty million from the university budget. As soon as the students came out in masses and demonstrated all over the city the Prime Minister turned to them and said "See, they are using

75

their feet and not their brains, all of them are stupid". He attacked the intellectual fraternity which was his main support for new ideas in revolutionizing the direction of the government. He started to attack his friends there. The students were very disillusioned. They started to say that their parents have lost income, they have suffered an additional tax after suffering a wage freeze..., their brothers and sisters have lost their food (school lunch programs were cut), and have lost their book rights (public school book subsidies were cut). And now the authorities expect the same children's parents to pay more in tuition to pay for them to get a secondary and a university education. People just can't take anymore, I know that I can't....

Many thousands have been driven below the poverty line in the last year, with retrenchments, with layoffs, with dismissals, with early retirement. People have been forced to accept these hardships as companies which sort of trim their work force with the drop in the price of oil. Then all of these conditions are added together. On top of that we impose a regime that doesn't care, that says, well, they know that Amoco has to export it's profits, they know that government authorities have to appease U.S. multinationals. By the way they adjusted Amoco's taxes in January, 1988. Just as they imposed the same tax on us they had to appease Amoco some more by cutting theirs. The government says we have to take these measures because we have nowhere else to go. That's what the Prime Minister told my union. We took a delegation to appeal to him to have some sympathy for the people of our country who have to live. We asked, "Why don't you repeal this tax measure because I know of many workers who are taking home minus dollars". So he said," I know these companies have to take out their money, and so I have to take it from the workers because I have to get it somewhere". He doesn't care how we live...

The masses have just had so much, that we question the Westminster system. We have tried it every five years since the twenties. I mean we have been working on it, and we give a new group a shot at it every five years, a new group of academics, a new group of business men, a new group of somebody, and they've all betrayed us. So change is coming.

What Can We Do?

Q.: (T. Turner) I think we have worked hard enough tonight, unless there is a pressing question, I'm thinking of a famous rap calypso from Trinidad called "Message to the Intellectuals from the Grassroots",...It's a rap calypso that deals with a challenge the singer raises for high-school students, university students, and young intellectuals. I was sitting here remarking that you and I were probably about the same age, and are the only two women that I can think of who were somehow working in the oil business, but for the worker, with the worker, as a worker. You raised the point about the need in your union for corporate research, for research assistance, for applied intellectual and research capacity. You mentioned that your television brings in these canned programs from Hollywood and elsewhere, and I was immediately thinking of one of the projects of some students of Smith to produce a video on Central American news coverage. It could be viewed as an alternative to Dallas. Could you say something about how you got to be doing what you are doing as an educator and as a researcher, in the organization, the Oilfields Workers Trade Union? C.L.R. James, the pan-Africanist, said about Trinidad's oil union in London on the occasion of his birthday in a public lecture that your union was the most remarkable and magnificent organization that the Caribbean peoples have hitherto produced. This fifty year old oil union in Trinidad inspired unionization in all of the British colonies. So I would be very interested in knowing how you got to be doing what you are doing as an educator, and what you think is the responsibility of the young intellectual.

DC: Well, I think we all have a contribution to make. Actually, we all have to do something with our knowledge. It's within our destiny to determine who we will serve. So you can either use your knowledge to further exploit people or help end exploitation. I remember when I was in Toronto there were two librarians, one of the librarians was a South African, and she and her husband were going to work for the apartheid government in South Africa. She was willing to put her knowledge at the disposal of the regime in power there, whereas I moved to Detroit and went in the opposite direction. I put my limited training at the disposal of the workers in Detroit. I worked in labor archives at the Wayne State University library where I got my masters. That was my laboratory for learning what contribution workers were making to the national income. Workers keep an economy churning, turning, and earning. These unseen numbers of people produced and contributed so much that they are never recognized for. Without them we intellec-

77

tuals wouldn't have a job. There wouldn't be white collar work if there was no blue collar work, although automation is now transforming many of us into automated collars not blue or white.That is always a struggle for us intellectuals, to decide what we are going to do with our knowledge, and whom is it going to serve. Will we become stock brokers at Merrill Lynch? Will we go Wall Street? Will we go in a classroom at Smith College and try to influence young minds? Just what will we do? Will we become self employed in our own business and employ people who we will exploit under whatever conditions? That is a decision you all have to make.

I think it is very important for you to decide before you leave here what you are going to do with your knowledge, who is it going to serve. You must feel confident with yourself in order to live with yourself and whatever decisions you make.... The untold millions who contribute to making America a powerful empire,they deserve your attention and they deserve your contributions.

Think about them some time. And the project with your grandmother's I was hearing about I am very interested in the experiment of some of Terisa's students who were interviewing grandmothers, concerning what their lives would have been like fifty years ago, when immigrant labor was being exploited, when Rockefeller was making more money off the Polish immigrants who built the railroads, who created the auto industries and empires here. They certainly deserve your attention. At home, I'm engaged in a oral history program to document the experiences of those people, the people who had to have a pass in Trinidad and Tobago to go from one department to another...(Pauses because of a noisy commotion coming from outdoors, near the lecture hall)...what was that?

From the audience: It's a Take Back the Night rally protesting violence against women, do you hear them, "No More Rape!, Stop Rape Now!".

DC: Yeah... we've had one of those at home... a night demonstration against violence ... maybe we should wind up and join them (general laughter).
But certainly this is a question I'd like to pose to you all as we wind up, that you think about it, about just what your going to do with your knowledge and your future.

GRAFFITI-PROPAGANDA
A HOW TO FOR THE FIRST OFFENDER

...S. OUT

...T IT WHERE
...OPLE CAN SEE IT.

LIKE INSIDE PHONE BOOTHS OR ACROSS FROM A BUS STOP

REVOL

REAL ESTATE

OR WHERE IT MAKES A POINT

WORK IN GROUPS WITH ONE PERSON AS LOOK-OUT

4 A.M. – 6 A.M. IS PRIME TIME. COPS CHANGE SHIFTS AT 5 A.M.

DON'T BE TOO CONSPICUOUS.

AT FIRST IT WILL SPRAY TOO THICK OR TOO THIN –

NOZZLES ARE INTERCHANGEABLE SOME SPRAY BETTER. SAVE THEM.

SO START THE CAN OUT ON AN UNIMPORTANT SURFACE.

A STENCIL IS A PIECE OF BOARD WITH HOLES CUT IN IT. BY SPRAYING THROUGH THE HOLES AN IMAGE

IS CREATED ON A SURFACE. THE STENCIL SHOULD BE TAPED TO THE SURFACE THE CAN, ABOUT 1 FT. AWAY.

...E CHEAPEST ...Y TO PRINT ...MALL # OF ...STERS ... XEROX, ...R A LARGE ...USE ...OFFSET

GLUE ON WITH A SOLUTION OF WATER & ELMERS GLUE OR WATER & WHEAT PASTE

IF SOLUTION IS THIN ENOUGH YOU CAN SRAY IT FROM A 'FANTASTIK' BOTTLE

COVER SURFACE WITH GLUE BEFORE YOU PUT ON POSTER.

STICK POSTER ON THEN SPRAY ON TOP OF IT TO SEAL IT.

ONT COVER SOME—
NE ELSES GRAFFITI.

BE SURE THERE
IS SOMEONE
TO CALL IF
ARRESTED

GRAFFITI IS A CRIME AGAINST
PROPERTY NOT PEOPLE SO
MAKE IT UPLIFTING.

THIS IS THE
CORNER WHER
MICHAEL STEW
WAS LYNCHED E
11 COPS (ALLEGEDLY
DOING GRAFFITI) ON
YEAR LATER IT
COVERED WITH A
-COP POSTERS A
ART. IF THE P
POSE OF KILLI
STEWART WA
TO DISCOURAC
PEOPLE FROI
DOING GRAFFI
IT DIDN'T
WORK

THE COVER-UP CONTINUES

REMEMBER MICHAEL STEWART

ON SEPT 15TH 1983 MICHAEL STEWART WAS ARRESTED FOR ALLEGEDY "WRITING GRAFFITTI ON A SUBWAY WALL" ELEVEN TRANSIT POLICE OFFICERS WERE SEEN KICKING & BEATING 25-YEAR-OLD STEWART'S BODY WHILE HANDCUFFED..... ONE WITNESS SAW STEWART BEING CHOKED WITH A NIGHTSTICK. HIS UNIDENTIFIED COMATOSE BODY WAS DUMPED AT BELLEVUE HOSP. WHERE HE DIED 13 DAYS LATER. THE MEDICAL EXAMINER ILLEGALLY REMOVED THE EYES FROM MICHAEL'S BODY, TO HIDE EVIDENCE OF STRANGULATION. ALL 11 COPS ARE STILL ON THE STREET WEARING THEIR BADGES.

81

NOV. 1984 A GROUP OF POLICE OFFICERS
WITH SHIELDS, BULLET-PROOF VESTS AND RIC
HELMETS BROKE DOWN THE DOOR ON 66 YE
OLD ELEANOR BUMPURS' BRONX APARTMENT
SHE TRIED TO DEFEND HERSELF WITH KITCHE
UTENSILS BUT THEY SHOT HER TWICE A
POINT BLANK RANGE WITH A SHOTGUN
THE POLICE HAD COME BECAUSE SHE WAS
LATE IN PAYING HER RENT.

POLICE STATE AMERICA

HY DO FOUR MEN NEED BULLETPROOF VESTS AND A
HOT GUN TO DEAL WITH AN OLD WOMAN? WHY IS
HE CITY READY TO SPILL BLOOD OVER THE
OLLECTION OF RENT? THESE PEOPLE ARE
CARED. THEY AND THE PEOPLE THEY WORK
OR, THE LANDLORDS AND CORPORATE HEADS
HO LIVE BEHIND BULLETPROOF GLASS, WILL
OT FEEL SAFE AS LONG AS THERE IS ONE
REE PERSON IN THE WORLD.
    HARD AS IT IS FOR US TO UNDERSTAND THIS
RUEL MURDER, IT MUST BE EVEN HARDER FOR THEM
O UNDERSTAND HOW ELEANOR BUMPURS COULD
TAND UP TO FOUR HEAVILY ARMED MEN. WE
NOW THAT ELEANOR WASN'T LEAVING HER
PARTMENT BECAUSE SHE DIDN'T HAVE ANOTHE
LACE TO GO. SHE HAD HER BACK TO THE WALL.

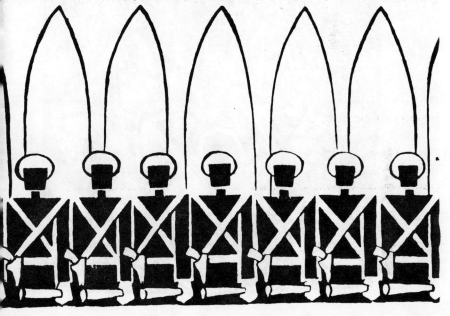

Painting by Ola Oladapo, tempera on cloth

Jamaican Farm Workers in the U.S.

Matthew J. Collins

I became interested in the state of U.S. farming when I moved to western Massachusetts and began working on a dairy farm in the winter of 1988. I am a senior at the University of Massachusetts. Because the nature of my study is progressive, I've tried to find progressive elements in U.S. farming. These "elements" can be seen in the Animal Rights movement or the crisis of the farmer in the U.S. midwest. A growing concern for the international dimensions of agriculture has led me to investigate migrant farm workers. Specifically I wanted to know more about contracted Jamaican farm workers in western New England.

Jamaican farm workers have been coming to U.S. farms for more than 15 years. They are employed for six to seven months out of the year, from about July to November. To find out first hand what migrants go through I met and became friends with three workers on a small farm in a small western New England town. I very much value knowing these men. They helped me a great deal in my inquiry and gave me new and exciting insights. I have changed their names out of consideration for their privacy. They are Francis, a forty year old farmer from the north east part of Jamaica; Thomas, a 28 year old carpenter from Kingston; and Vincent; a 45 year old man of jovial disposition who has spent his whole life as a contracted farm worker. I will call their boss Larry. I owe them a lot. I am trying to describe these men's experience from their perspective and in their interests.

Modern Slavery

The condition of the Jamaican farm worker in the U.S. is a condition of modern slavery. Jamaica is plagued by underdevelopment caused by hard-dying imperialism. From the 1600s when the British brought African slaves to produce sugar in Jamaica to the late 1900s, foreigners have extracted wealth from Jamaica. Exported wealth includes both products and the labor power of migrant workers. The wealth is concentrated in London and other industrial capitals of the world. This leaves the majority of Jamaican people at home penniless.

Natural catastrophe, on top of economic catastrophe, has further traumatized the lives of the Jamaican people. The 1988 hurricane Gilbert pulverized the tiny society. A people who traditionally rely on agriculture for domestic consumption, are now left without their only recourse. Bananas, yams, sugar cane, squashes, plantains, and coconuts are among the commonly grown crops. All farms have been damaged and returning them to full production will be very difficult. Arboreal agriculture is perhaps the most severely affected by the hurricane. For instance when a banana tree is knocked down it takes five years for the tree to grow again to maturity.

Jamaica with its 2.2 million people, is a Caribbean island half the size and half the population of Massachusetts. It is located south of Cuba and east of Haiti. Its economic booms and busts have been orchestrated by British colonial business, and since World War II, by U.S. corporate interests. Jamaica is squarely within the imperialism network. The sugar, bauxite and gypsum are valuable resources which have kept foreign capital interested in the country. The colony gained its full independence from the United Kingdom in 1962. In 1972 many Jamaicans foresaw the possibility of some kind of economic 'independence' (or at least more leverage in a new set of interdependent relations). Michael Manley was elected prime minister of Jamaica in that year. The new government proceeded to take over the major industries which were privately owned (bauxite, sugar and gypsum). Foreign capital was no doubt aggravated by this a move. With the aid of their home governments, the corporations forced Manley out and inserted a prime minister who was anything but a militant in third world affairs. Edward Seaga was elected in 1980 and governs to this day. He is pro-capitalist and committed to maintaining the status-quo. Fundamental change, however, is urgently needed in this country of high unemployment and high inflation.

Tourism has been one of the biggest of Jamaica's industries, in terms of generating foreign exchange. Jamaican citizens with whom I spoke were in favor of tourists because of the cash they bring. Nevertheless, there is inevitably some resentment of tourists. I was extremely impressed by the spirit and humanity of the Jamaicans that I met. They were first of all amiable, courteous folks. They were sincerely interested in educating and corresponding with the me. They frequently emphasized the oneness of the world's people. The migrant workers were deliberate about discussing that point with me. The pro-peace international outlook which these Jamaicans expressed was spiritually uplifting.

Terms of International Labor Contracts

The economic illness of Jamaica has surely to do with its addiction to foreign capital. Jamaica's elite (business people, professionals, government bureaucrats, drug dealers and big property owners) are middlemen between international capital and ordinary, exploited Jamaicans. To deal with the problem of high unemployment, Jamaica's ruling class has turned to foreigners for assistance. The capitalists at the helm of business and the state in Jamaica have joined with U.S. agrocapitalists in a mutually beneficial relation. Their solution is for Jamaican labor to be exploited not in their own country but on U.S. soil.

The United States and the Jamaican governments have struck a deal in which the Jamaican government will provide temporary contracted labor to work on U.S. farms for approximately half of the year. The terms of the contract reflect the low bargaining power of the Jamaican government. The workers are to be paid $5.10 per hour regardless of the number of hours or type of work. Housing and transportation are provided but the laborers buy their own food and whatever other supplies they might need. There are no benefits for the Jamaicans comparable those that every other U.S. employee expects. U.S. workers have fought hard for and won Social Security, welfare, unemployment insurance, workman's compensation, medicaid and a relatively high standard of living. However, even though some of the contracted Jamaican farmers may spend half of each year of their working lives producing wealth in the U.S., they do not see these benefits.

Their employers and the U.S. government have found a way to sneak around such decent forms of compensation. This reality may come as a shock to some. The popular image of the U.S. farmer is not consistent with the practice of such abuse. After all, he/she has been one of the worst affected by the economy and environment of our time. But the world of the family farm is not the world of agribusiness based on migrant labor. The farmers hiring Jamaican citizens are not the ones who are about to lose their farms to foreclosure. Rather, they are huge sugar cane farmers in Florida, the tobacco industry in the South and in Connecticut and the commercial orchards of New England in the northeast. These owners of agribusinesses claim that they cannot find U.S. labor to employ, and yet here we have unemployment. When U.S. workers cannot be attracted by minimum wages to arduous farm labor, foreign workers are brought in from societies driven to the crisis point by imperialism and international recession. The truth is the U.S.farmer is getting quite a deal. The situation can be likened to feudalism. The Jamaican citizens do service to their U.S. 'lords' for half of each year. Having done their time they return to Jamaica to use their savings on their own small farms or businesses.

What contractual form does modern slavery take? What deal is struck between governments as they trade across national boundaries in that potent commodity, labor power? In Jamaica men interested in earning U.S. dollars (one U.S. dollar is worth five times one Jamaican dollar) must submit an application to the Jamaican Ministry of Labor. One migrant worker explained that "If you know the political boss in your parish then your application is considered, and you are subjected to a physical examination." The physical exam tests your dexterity, strength, and health. The Jamaicans I spoke to told me that the dexterity part was emphasized. Presumably those who have good dexterity make good pickers. If you pass all these tests then you enter a pool of available farmers. The majority of Jamaicans who come to work on U.S. farms are farmers themselves and so are already skilled. Others are tradesmen and their skills as mechanics and craftsmen are eagerly exploited by U.S. employers.

The process continues overseas. In the U.S. farm owners apply through the Department of Labor in Washington D.C. for a certain number of workers. The agribusinessman signs a contract which stipulates that:
1. the Jamaicans are to be paid $5.10 per hour (U.S.);
2. monthly allowances will be given equal to half of their weekly earnings (the rest of their pay will be given to them when they return

to Jamaica);

3. the American farm owners will provide transportation to and from Jamaica and adequate housing in the U.S.; and

4. a member of the Jamaican consulate will visit the farms frequently to assure the employers' compliance with the contract.

What does it mean for the Jamaican farm worker to sign this contract? He is surrendering himself to these terms for the duration of his stay. Any complaint, any worker demonstration, anything but devoted obedience will mean deportation back to Jamaica. In my study I heard only of one instance of worker unrest. I had the opportunity to meet with the Jamaican intellectual and novelist, Erna Brodber, in Amherst in late 1988. She said that she remembered fellow parishioners being sent home from working in the United States because of some kind of disturbance. Those deported insisted that the disturbance was created by a group of contract laborers from another country. The U.S. also contracts Puerto Ricans, other Caribbean people, Chinese and Vietnamese to work on U.S. farms.

Earning U.S. dollars is considered a privilege by Jamaicans. Many are willing to endure the hardship that signing the contract entails. With U.S. dollars they can afford to live better than most other Jamaicans even though they only work half of the year. One Jamaican migrant farm worker told me "I have four children, a farm, and a wife, I can't afford to be saying to Larry, 'look boss the work is hard, I want some more money' he'd say 'Jamaica!'". Francis, Thomas, and Vincent all emphasized the fact that they had signed a contract and so were obligated to obey. They know that they are treated like wageslaves. But these men are willing to subject themselves to semi-slavery because it is the best strategy open to them to get ahead and to support a family back in Jamaica. What happens to their wages? Farm workers eagerly try to increase their standard of material living by buying toys such as V.C.R.s, T.V.s and stereos. More importantly the money goes to sustain their families and to support their personal farms or businesses.

Work Conditions

While in the U.S. the Jamaicans work hard. A ten hour day for six days out of the week is the norm. Most of the men are farmers already

89

and their skill is extremely valuable to their employers. In fact many of the crops grown on New England farms are also grown by Jamaicans on their own farms in-the Caribbean. Francis pointed out that just as his boss Larry employs him to bring in the harvest, Francis has to hire men in order to keep his farm in Jamaica going.

The housing provided for migrants is deplorable. One New England orchard in the community I studied, was prevented by the U.S. Department of Labor from accepting the Jamaican employees it requested. Housing provided for the farm workers did not comply with some simple regulations such as the provision of linen, curtains, and adequate bathing facilities. The typical abode is a barracks. The group of farm workers that I met lived in a very shabby old house that their employer had rented for them. Plans are now in the making to build new barracks to house these men as well as those employed by other local farm owners. News of these plans has aroused protest among the townspeople of this small western Massachusetts farming community. Fears of increased crime and decreasing property values are the main complaints.It is evident that deep-rooted prejudices are at the bottom of the uneasiness of the townspeople. After all the Jamaicans have been coming to this area for years. In a newspaper article about the situation a local police chief stated that "We haven't associated any crime with the Jamaican workers ever."

Runaways

Earning U.S. dollars is what these men are after. A black market exists to help them continue earning, not under contracts but with citizenship. Some Jamaicans run away from their U.S. employers to whom they are contracted. They flee to the cities where the black market helps them to find wives who are U.S. citizens. A non-citizen gets permanent resident status (the green card) once married to a citizen. American women are recruited (some are even approached on the street) and offered money to temporarily marry a non-U.S. citizen. The marriage last only long enough for the alien to become an official citizen. Then the couple gets a divorce. If the man has a family back home he may then send for them. Erna Brodber told me of one of her fellow parishioners who had just run away from his employer in the U.S. This escapee married and divorced. Soon he would be sending for his family. Thomas told me that two men had run away from Larry's farm for the same reason. From U.S. employers' point of view, importing non-citizens provides labor at a cost which is less than employing citizens. Migrants can be disciplined by the threat of deportation. Citizens have much more power than migrants in the boss-worker relationship. Being a migrant farm worker may fit into a strategy aimed at increasing wages and benefits (including social amenities and services) for the Jamaican individual and his entire family.

Life for the Jamaican men in the U.S. is very lonely. Although they live with their countrymen, these Jamaicans are not family or fellow parishioners. The work is extremely hard physical labor. Especially difficult is the work in the sugar cane fields of southern Florida. "It was the hardest, most awful work I ever done", Francis told me. Work days for the men I met last ten to fourteen hours and yet the wage remains $5.10 per hour regardless of hours worked. There is no overtime. After a killing day, the men go home to prepare their own Caribbean style meals. In some cases (or for holidays) the migrant workers' food is prepared by the wives and mothers of the farm owners. If the Jamaicans get sick or injured they go back home. Then the burden of nursing and replenishing their labor power falls on the women of their families. The employer pays only for the hours at work. It is women here and especially in Jamaica, who re-fuel and repair the worker. These women are not paid, but get only those benefits that men see fit and are able to give. This reinforces men's economic power over women. We can see why the agribusinessmen in the U.S. get such low-cost farm labor. Women in Jamaica serve and in fact produce the migrant, but for no (or very little) pay . Our low-priced fruit and vegetables are being subsidized by the unpaid work of Jamaican families from which semi-slave farm workers come. Of course, the agricapitalists in the U.S. make higher profits from this international system of low pay and no pay.

This perspective on migrant labor has implications for any agenda to end sexism, racism and class exploitation. U.S. farm owners have internationalized the labor market for fruit and vegetable pickers. Jamaican migrants, by their production and presence in the U.S., connect us to the production and the culture of Jamaica. We can act to solidify these connections, and most U.S. citizens who have started to do so are drawn into unity through reggae, brought into this country by migrant workers from Jamaica and other Caribbean countries.

Reggae and Internationalism

In the Pioneer Valley of western Massachusetts there is one place for Jamaican farm workers to turn for comfort and company. At this place people of different races, sexes and classes gather and have fun; and in the process we undermine racism, sexism and class division. We move to replace them with international friendship. Yvonne's Caribbean Restaurant in Hadley, Massachusetts is the sight of this most progressive process. It happens whenever Yvonne has a reggae party, which is usually once a month. At one of these parties you may find white middle class students, Jamaican farm workers, university professors, international students, Afro-American students and working men and women.

Yvonne is a remarkable woman. She was born in Guyana to a black mother (African and French) and a Jewish caucasian father. She migrated from Guyana to the U.S. She raised nine children and sent them all to university with money she earned by her own hard work. "I did everything starting from scrubbing floors." She herself has obtained an undergraduate and a masters degree in Food Science and Nutrition, and is now pursuing a doctorate in multi-cultural education.

If you go to Yvonne's on a night she's having a party you're sure to participate in a multicultural experience. I went to one of Yvonne's reggae parties for the first time as part of my investigation into Jamaican farm workers. That night I met and had the most delightful conversations with some very diverse people. They included a professor from Senegal, a Mexican-American student, a Jamaican farm worker and an Afro-American student. People of all ages were there getting along with one another. They were dancing to reggae, calypso and soca, eating Yvonne's famous 'Caribbean soul' food, drinking her fruit juices and her Red Stripe beer.

Yvonne's reggae parties provide an experience that is revolutionary because it subverts the dividing forces of racism, sexism and classism that are so obviously part of our world. This is evident from the words of the people who I talked to at the party. Francis told me, "We are all one people, one love brother." Yvonne, in her beautiful accent echoed these words, "If I cut you, you will not bleed white, and if you cut me I will not bleed black. Here you have the white man dancing with the black woman and the white woman dancing with the black man and nobody cares." Professor Diop from Senegal said of the reggae parties, "People come for different reasons: the Jamaicans for a taste of home, the white student for the music, but what they take home is worth much more." Thomas, the Mexican-American student was ecstatic about what was going on. "Man, this is great!" he exclaimed.

I agree. Those who attend parties at Yvonne's take part in multi-national culture. They relate in a healthy, joyful atmosphere, to people different from them socially or racially. With this experience they go back to their lives like ambassadors of good will. The affect of Yvonne's parties is far reaching. Besides the variety of patrons who are U.S. citizens, many other nationalities are represented there. Jamaican farm workers will go home and know how welcome is Jamaican culture within the U.S. where it makes us more internationally oriented. Graduates from Yvonne's ' school of multicultural education' will build unity and understanding among we who have been divided. And all of this happens through Caribbean culture, rooted now in western Massachusetts.

The case of the Jamaican farm worker in the United States is a curious one. Men are transported a thousand miles from their homes and they are paid very little. The burden of replenishing their labor power lies with the women associated with the U.S. farms and the women in their lives at their homes in Jamaica. With their presence at Yvonne's, a potential for international, intercultural solidarity is created. The emergence of a socialist world is characterized by the strengthening of this international communication and understanding. As we come to know the Jamaican men and their struggle and they come to know us, we both recognize that we are allies. Our common enemy is capital, exploiting our labor and resources. We recognize that our common goals are peace, egalitarianism and health. To put it plainly and simply; we all want, need, and together can win the struggle to have a good life.

People's Education in South Africa

John Hanson

Move To Resist

I am student at the University of Massachusetts at Amherst, majoring in Social Thought and Political Economy. I come from a white, working class family. My grandfather is from Sweden, but my mother's people came from Britain over a hundred years ago. I was born and grew up in Hyde Park, Boston, the last of six children. I am interested in what is happening socially and politically in the Third World. It seems like more is happening there in terms of revolutionary culture than is happening here.

I am interested in education in revolution. Education should develop our minds and bodies to their fullest capacity. I chose to study education in South Africa because the society is based on inequality between whites who rule and blacks who are ruled. Also state violence, racism, sexism and class exploitation are extreme. Official education is reproducing these inequalities and is blocking the development of black South Africans. And yet a tremendous social upheaval is now underway in apartheid South Africa. What is it within black South African culture that is transforming the process of people's education?

This work owes much to the education I received from South African people, to Terisa's hard-driving editing and to Ingrid Bracey's guidance.

South African Illusion

A cloud of dust
and through it seen
black native dancing around
a fire
surrounded by straw and bamboo huts

and in the distance
a cloud of dust
and through it seen
herds of elephants
and on the horizon
the sun is setting:
National Geographic.
Dutch sailed to the Cape and
kicked these Africans out:
a lesson in high school on
the colonization of South Africa.
The white man made
to look just like me
could only have brought
good news
and good things.
The white man trades
and prays
and self-defends,
while the black,
inferior,
devil native steals
and murders
and kicks up the flames of hell.
We
are
all
created
equal
but separate:
new idea.
Black
Africans placed in a homeland.

Black
natives thrusting each other
with the sharp spear of
bitter historical rivalry yet
dulled by colonization.
1948: advancing industrialized nation.
A fight against communism.
White
minority supreme,
Black
focus on that theme.
Black
second class citizens.
Black
wielding AK-47,
second class citizen communists.
The ANC,
a bunch of terrorists supported by Russia.
The PAC,
black
no cream or sugar.
Freeeeeee Nelson Mandela!
Biko
because Biko.
The white police using
plastic bullets,
water hoses,
truncheons,
tear gas,
dogs,
one reel says Alabama
another says South Africa.
I heard

Gandhi was
in South Africa.
I heard
Martin Luther King Jr. followed
in Gandhi's footsteps.
Jesus Christ
There is
gold,
silver,
uranium,
a global scramble for scarce resources:
the main gist.
U.S. divests its name,
yet leases its game.
  Where exploitation exists,
U.S.A. or South Africa,
move to resist.

Education and social change

South Africa's white government has long run a school system which keeps blacks in their place. Black resistance has posed an alternative educational process which champions liberation. The strategy and tactics of confronting racist, Bantu education contribute to making a new type of human being and a new type of society in South Africa. In what follows I describe the education system white rulers have devised for black people. I show how a people's education grew out of apartheid education. Finally I consider the methods by which black students are educating themselves.

Bantu (that is, racist) education is one way that the South African state shapes and controls black workers. The Bantu education system is part of official institutional culture. A key purpose is to orient the black South African to the white view of the world. This orientation is necessary because black culture provides ideas and inspiration which

97

undermine the strategy of white power. Mokubung O. Nkomo, a black South African educator, observed in 1981 that black people's education "has developed a culture of its own which is at odds with the official intentions." Social upheaval engages students who form the most politically volatile section of society. Mokubung suggested that "forces external to in-class instruction have exerted as great an influence as the official curriculum." These forces make up what Mokubung calls the 'culture of resistance,' and it is people's education which reproduces the resistance. Before considering the culture of resistance I review the history of official education and its role in the overall political, economic and cultural makeup of South Africa.

Official Education Strategies for Blacks

In 1948, the Afrikaner Nationalist Party rose to power and implemented the system of apartheid. Apartheid is a systematic and determined policy of racial segregation. It is a complex of regulations, laws and decrees that govern the day to day activities of the various racial and ethnic groups. These rules define the territorial divisions of South Africa along racial and ethnic lines.

Why was the systematic imposition of apartheid necessary in the post World War II period? The central concerns of white governments after 1948 were to protect white workers from encroachment by blacks on the job and in the community, to decrease the number of blacks in white areas and to curb the economic mobility of blacks through pass laws and a stricter enforcement of the color bar. These policies maintained white power, and the profits of white South African and international corporations, especially in mining.

Before 1948, the idea existed in South African official circles that the Europeans and the "natives" (whites and blacks) should 'develop separately'. This meant a kind of semi-slavery for blacks, enforced by drastic segregation, and dispossession of blacks. The Land Act of 1913 set aside 13 percent of the land as reservations (homelands!) for black South Africans. Indigenous Africans were forced into these reservations according to their ancestry. Frederickson states that "the architects of the land act of 1913 had not envisioned a total and permanent partition of the population. In fact their main concern was to increase the supply of labor available to white farmers and industrialists by stifling the incipient growth of an African peasant class outside the reserved area." (George Frederickson, *White Supremacy*, Oxford. 1981; 244)

In order to maintain the unequal distribution of land and wealth, to restrict access to jobs and to exclude black South Africans from the political process outside of the homelands; the South African government needs a large army and police force. But it also needs the official culture to orient blacks and to give credence to the idea of separate development or apartheid. The official culture has many dimensions. It is the religion which condemns 'native' religions as devil worshipping and it is the scientific claims that blacks are genetically inferior. Official culture is also the education system.

The Bantu Education Act was adopted in 1953. Its aim, according to Mokubung, was to educate Africans about their ethnic identities and to provide basic literacy and numeracy skills needed by an expanding economy. From the early 1950s the purpose of Bantu education was "to direct the education of Africans so as to meet the needs of an economy dominated by a white racial oligarchy and to train African personnel to manage various administrative sectors of the homelands and ethnic institutions in the 'white' areas in furtherance of the policy of separate development." (Mokubung O. Nkomo, *Student Culture in Black South African Universities*. Thesis (Ed. D.) University of Mass, 1983: 127.)

Ways of Resistance

The culture of resistance can be seen early in the history of Dutch colonization when African tribes such as the Khoikhoi resisted the encroaching Boers. Zulus warred against the invading English. The African National Congress (ANC) was formed in 1912 to resist separate development and to oppose white seizure of black people's lands. The ANC stood against the Union of South Africa which meant a union of white power. This state was consolidating its control of diverse and frequently divided black Africans. The ANC went to Versailles in 1919 after World War i in an attempt to be recognized as the representative of blacks in South Africa and gain legitimation in the eyes of the world powers. But the question of blacks received almost no attention from colonial powers.

In the inter-war period Europe and the USA were preparing for the next round of competition to control Third World markets, resources and labor. It wasn't until after World War II and the emergence of black nationalism that the world powers and the United Nations dealt seriously with the question of independence for colonized non-European peoples. Then white South Africa rallied to support the Afrikaner Nationalist Party and its agenda of apartheid. This agenda gave more sophisticated answers to the questions about why blacks were not sharing in the fruits of the land.

In 1960 the Pan African Congress (PAC) was formed as an off-shoot of the ANC. The PAC stance was one of consolidating black power against white supremacy. The PAC came to the conclusion that nonviolent demonstration and diplomacy were not working and that the use of armed revolution was a necessary means to overthrow the oppressive apartheid regime. The ANC followed this line but maintained an organization that also included whites.

Over the decades the ANC, PAC, and other organizations have set up schools to teach their revolutionary programs. But it was not until the mid 1970s that the idea of using the official education system as a tool to augment and support the revolution gained force. The culture of resistance had deepened to the point that blacks were supplementing or even replacing the official curriculum with people's education.

Soweto

In June 1976, school children in Soweto protested the use of Afrikaans as the main language for education. This had long been a contentious issue: English education meant advancement for blacks. In the early 1970's the government was making a move to phase out the use of English and teach only Afrikaans. There are four required subjects, two of which were always taught in English and two in Afrikaans. Students are also taught their native languages. The Afrikaners were making a move to push out the English to consolidate state control This policy could strengthen an "Afrikaans Only" movement.

The Soweto uprising of 1976, was a spontaneous rejection and refusal of Afrikaner cultural and political resurgence. An important aspect of the Soweto demonstration which differentiates it from earlier protests is that school children of six to twelve years were the participants. At this age, most black South African children have not been fully conditioned into an acceptance of the Afrikaner psychology. And many of the school children were especially militant because they had few vested interests; they had nothing to lose.

On June 16th there was a demonstration of hundreds of students in the township of Soweto. A student activist, Tsietsi Mashinini and many others did the political work to get people involved in the non-violent protest. (Black Africans say that you will grow to fulfill your name: Tsietsi is translated 'trouble'.) The school children were met with repression. Police fired on the school children, killed hundreds, and detained hundreds more. The Soweto uprising carried on into the next few weeks. Unfortunately for the students the uprising took place with the school year about to end. The school semester runs from January to June and July to November. It was expected the government would give in to the demands but the Afrikaners held firm and the following semester the students came back and were better organized. When the schools reopened there were more shootings. The death toll was in the hundreds by November 1976, at the end of this school semester. There were ripple effects from the Soweto uprising into other townships. According to one black South African, who spoke with me, "They experienced it slowly, there was fear, it was something new, some kind of dawn of a new era. It meant life or death. The government came in and it was like putting yourself in front of a firing squad."

The government gave the people a reason to rise up by taking a deeply felt educational issue and imposing an official position. Then the stated showed itself to be all out to kill. Black people then rallied around the deaths of the children. The issue grew out from a demand for the cancellation of Afrikaans, to a concern for the deaths of students, to the release of the students who were detained. The Student Representative Council (SRC) was set up to act as a mouthpiece for students to negotiate with the school system. Soon the issue broadened

Hector Petersen, the first child to be shot dead by police in Soweto on 16 June 1976

Photographer: Sam Nzima, courtesy of International Defence and Aid Fund for Southern Africa

Soweto children protest

Photo by Peter Magubane, courtesy of the International Defence and Aid Fund for Southern Africa

Tony McGrath

In a rural area

to encompass all apartheid relations. Negotiation will not end until apartheid ends. The Soweto Student Committee was formed to develop support and solidarity in the surrounding community. This committee deals with issues of local concern. For instance, if there is a death of a student, then money would be collected or if a family didn't want their children to participate in the demonstrations then there would be an attempt to change the minds of the parents. The state applied pressure on the parents of students to keep the students in line. This created a lot of conflict and a Parents Crisis Committee was organized to give support to those that are feeling the pressure.

People's Education

It was out of the Soweto uprising that the student movement adopted a strategy to politicize the blacks through the school system. Most other areas outside of Johannesburg joined in the movement in 1977. Consciousness raising was not unique in Soweto. Other areas had already begun a black consciousness movement on their own, more out of a natural impulse to the oppressive system. And there was the Black Consciousness Movement (BCM) which existed in theory before 1976. But it was not until the Soweto uprising that the black consciousness movement really began serious practice.

Many student activists began what they called "conscientization" (con-she-en-shiz-a-shun). This is politicization. It is education which supplements or exists outside the official education. Conscientization is also called "people's education." The students have had some success introducing people's education in the classroom. A South African said that students would ask teachers, who are also black, about black Africans' history and struggles. If the teacher refused to teach these subjects, the students would ask the teacher to leave so they could have their own discussions. Black high school students are holding their own discussions about the PAC and the ANC and have renamed their high schools. For example, one school is Nelson Mandela High. A popular slogan is 'Liberation now, education later'. A South African student told me that another slogan says 'let's push the Boers into the Indian ocean.' She explained that the idea of pushing the Boers into the ocean reflects immaturity. In fact, she said, both the ANC and the PAC (although the PAC may be a black only organization) want all those that participate in the overthrow of apartheid to participate in the decision making process of a new society. The students, through the SRC are trying to get the South African government to recognize people's education and the students are trying to infuse it into the surrounding communities.

People's education is designed to conscientize (pronounced con-shen-tize), or deepen popular understanding of the movement and of the overall revolution. People's education teaches the history of black Africans, their heros and struggles. It fills in the missing links. It gives new meaning to official concepts. It is aimed at involving people, breaking the cultural silence, and opening avenues through which people can contribute to change.

People's education re-examines the history of conflict between the Boers (the Dutch invaders) and indigenous people. In the history books Africans are presented as murderers and thieves whereas the encroaching Boers are portrayed as worthy pioneers acting in self defense. The history of the ANC and its leaders, including Mandela, Mbeke, and Sisulu, is taught. Terminology is examined for its real meaning. A word such as terrorism which is applied by the state to the ANC and the PAC is redefined. The ANC had long used nonviolent means trying to get its message out. But members and supporters were met by state terrorism and thus have chosen armed revolution as a last resort. Thus conscientization, the process of coming to political under-standing, is preparing South Africans for the taking of power.

How does conscientization treat relations between women and men? One black South African man told me that the general view in South Africa is that "Women are the strength of the home." He con-tinued by explaining that this is not meant "in the same sense that Western culture may say the women's place is in the kitchen. In South Africa the family has been broken by the governments' manipulation of the work force. This system with its pass laws brings men into the urban areas while not allowing wives and children to accompany them."

Black women have to struggle very hard to survive and to raise children who themselves witness and participate in their mothers' struggles. It is in this sense that black South Africans affirm that women are the strength of the home. This strength is found in the music. One song contains the line "when you strike the women you strike the rock." Black women sang this song when they demonstrated against the government's decision that women should carry passes.

Conscientization may at first not have had a special emphasis on women's concerns. Nor may it have addressed relations between women and men. But direct political action such as the rent boycotts or the refusal of squatters at Crossroads to move has demonstrated the tenacity of women. State repression of children has mobilized mothers. Women's struggles and the parts played by women in every facet of the South African revolution now have a much higher profile. In the 1987 miner's strike women medical workers operated a communications network. This informal communications system contributed fundamentally to the National Union of Miners' success. There are also changes in domestic relations. For instance, more often now men as well as women prepare food: "It depends who gets home first," a black South African woman told me. Nevertheless the view does persist that racism and class-based exploitation take precedence over sexism. In this view women's rights or gender-based exploitation are issues not for the moment but for after the achievement of black majority rule. As the anti-apartheid struggle continues, this view comes under growing scrutiny.

Conscientization has been going on in South Africa for almost twenty years. It, along with dramatic political events, has forged an aware, militant and optimistic population. This is reflected in organizational flexibility. In the eighties the United Democratic Front was formed to act as a central organization for all the anti-apartheid organizations. The government has placed blanket bans on organizations, only to witness the springing up of new organizations. South Africa is the only industrialized society in which union membership has expanded in the 1980's. COSATU, the Congress of South African Trade Unions, was founded in 1984 and has successfully undertaken several national strikes. If blacks refuse to work South Africa stops. Consumer and rent boycotts have brought results. They have also enabled all South Africans to assess the power of self-organized blacks. In 1987 an underground students organization was founded. In contrast, official organizations such as the military are increasingly divided. In 1988 several hundred white draftees faced jail rather than go into the military to fight against blacks in South Africa, Namibia, Mozambique or Angola.

Political transformation in South Africa has been so profound that white society is now divided. The far right advocates stricter apartheid. At the other end of the spectrum hundreds of whites have cast their lot with the black struggle. Those in the middle embrace reform. The South African government has acknowledged the importance and threat of people's education. The government is trying to absorb the dynamics of people's education into the rigid official culture. But it is unlikely that cosmetic reforms or co-optation will work. The longer the struggle continues, the greater are the determination and unity among South Africans at the bottom. This unity bridges divisions within South Africa, and increasingly abroad. We are being brought together across divides based on race, gender, and nationality. Peoples education, forged in the South African struggle, is now a tool for our use and for the use of our sisters and brothers everywhere in the world.

Blue Collar Asian Women

Photograph courtesy of Helaine Victoria Press and Joan W. Biren

Soweto children use dustbin shields against police bullets

Photographer: Peter Magubane, courtesy of the Internaitonal Defence and Aid Fund for Southern Africa

Photocopy of a T-shirt made in Trinidad in 1986 by the Committee In Defense of West Indian Cricket to protest matches involving British cricketers who had played in South Africa. "How Many More Must Die?" is a hit song.

"NOW YOU HAVE TOUCHED THE WOMEN

FREE AFRICA

YOU HAVE STRUCK A ROCK YOU HAVE DISLODGED A BOULDER YOU WILL BE CRUSHED"

"The Death of Apartheid"   FAITH RINGGOLD

The U.S. Anti-Apartheid Movement

Janine Cardello

Apartheid is a system of racial segregation that has a legislative base. The term "apartheid" was first used in 1944 by D.F. Malan, leader of South Africa's Nationalist opposition party. Malan claimed that a policy of separation was necessary "to insure the safety of the white race and of Christian civilization by the honest maintenance of the principles of apartheid and guardianship."[1] Under the apartheid system, whites subordinate blacks in an overt and severe way.

In South Africa, race tends to pre-determine class. The Black Consciousness of Steve Biko was based on this virtual identity of race and class. Those born black are condemned to live at the service of whites. Other options are not open to black people in South Africa. However, the white authorities, led by big business are trying to lure certain blacks into the middle class. The idea is to create a stratum of blacks with a commitment to the status quo and an interest in suppressing rebellion by the dispossessed majority.

To enforce this bizarre system, the South African Government has to draw sharp lines between people on the basis of physical appearance and family connections. For instance, hair texture is used as a means of classification. All South African people must carry identification with them at all times that states their race category. Black people must have special permission, stamped on their 'passes' to give them permission to live, move about in and work in cities.

Social segregation is harsh in South Africa. The facilities that are most affected by strict separation by race are government buildings, including post offices and police stations. These were either totally segregated or had partitions erected in them so that whites could be served on one side and blacks on the other. Other facilities that must be segregated are liquor outlets, civic halls, libraries, parks, theaters, cinemas, hotels, restaurants, cafes and clubs when they are located in the white areas. Apartheid infringes upon all dimensions of black South African existence. The white South African government has no com-

111

mitment to improving black people's conditions of life. The authorities justify the unequal allocation of resources to whites and blacks by defining black citizens as residents of 'different countries,' which are the so-called 'homelands.'

Apartheid has always been resisted by black South Africans with the support of a few whites. But in the last twenty years this resistance has grown to huge proportions. It is certain that black majority rule will, in a few years, be a reality in South Africa. As black struggle intensified, so has international support. Probably the best way that anti-apartheid positions can be pursued outside South Africa is through breaking economic and cultural links with the racist regime.

Until the end of the U.S. civil war, slavery and race-based discrimination were the rule in the United States. While racism is, as James Baldwin said, "alive and very unwell" in many societies worldwide, South Africa presents an extreme case. It is the only society in today's world in which the state enforces different treatment of people based solely on their color. The United States government and its allies in Japan, the United Kingdom and France support the South African apartheid regime. This alliance with a system which infringes on basic human rights can be explained in part by economic connections. European, U.S. and Japanese multinational corporations make especially high profits from the labor of black workers in South Africa. Growing numbers of citizens of western countries are opposed to the subordination of human rights to private profit under apartheid.

In this context a campaign has been mounted to enforce economic sanctions against South Africa. One of the goals is to put pressure on the South African Government to end apartheid. Another is to end South African military occupation of neighboring Namibia. However, U.S. administrations have vehemently opposed economic sanctions. Reagan has called them "immoral". He and British Prime Minister, Margaret Thatcher contend that economic sanctions will only hurt black South Africans. According to Reagan, the victims of a South African boycott would be the black workers. The mine workers would feel the greatest impact of economic sanctions, he has said, and the mine workers are mostly black. It is necessary to recognize that the U.S. Government can not be depended upon to directly oppose apartheid via economic sanctions.

Most anti-apartheid activists in the U.S. oppose economic dealings with South Africa. And since we can not rely on direct economic sanctions, enforced by the U.S. government, indirect methods must be used. The strategy involves convincing institutions with investments or other interests in firms that deal with South Africa to put pressure on those firms to sever ties with apartheid. The most common institutional investors have been churches, labor unions, universities, student associations, foundations, insurance companies, and state and local governments.

Churches, especially Protestant denominations, have become important participants in economic disengagement. The Episcopal Church, the United Church of Christ, and the United Methodist Church have historically been among the most active groups in the movement. The Interfaith Center on Corporate Responsibility (ICCR) coordinates and organizes many anti-apartheid church activities. The ICCR conducts social profiles on corporations and explores alternative investment opportunities for corporations. It guides particular churches in fulfilling resolutions they have made, such as ending an investment or asking for information that activists have been unable to obtain elsewhere. These initiatives are forms of shareholder activism.

In the 1980s churches have been joined by universities or state pension funds. In early 1982 the American Lutheran Church and eight other organizations, including the California Public Employee Retirement System and the California Teachers Retirement System, sponsored a resolution to prevent Xerox corporation from expanding its operations in South Africa or selling its products to the police and military. Combined support resulted in the resolution receiving ten percent of the shareholders' votes, representing some 1.5 million shares.

The economic boycott of South Africa is an issue on most U.S. university and college campuses. Students and faculty have pressured their institutions' boards of trustees to sell the South African related securities in the investment portfolios of endowment funds. This technique has worked well. Our own University of Massachusetts established a policy for divestment in 1977 and in 1984 had divested six million dollars from three corporations. The student co-op system at the University of California at Berkeley withdrew its accounts totaling four million dollars from Bank America in 1979, to protest that bank's participation in loans to South Africa.

Anti-apartheid activists give great importance to convincing state and local government to join the divestment effort. This is because state governments have large deposits in banks, they purchase goods and services, and they have responsibility for regulating large investments for state employees' pension funds and state university endowments. Cities also have large bank deposits, purchasing power and in a few cases, have financial holdings for pension funds. Obviously, state and local governments have more power to influence corporations to divest from South Africa than have universities.

The U.S. anti-apartheid movement has also succeeded in having Congress and the Senate pass sanctions legislation prohibiting certain economic and other interactions with South Africa. However, the federal administration has somewhat neutralized the impact of this legislation, using bureaucratic means. In 1985 the "Free South Africa" movement swept college campuses. But its impact was curtailed by press censorship in South Africa, and by tacit cooperation from the U.S. media. When political turmoil in South Africa was dramatized on U.S. television screens each evening, a national mobilization began to build. Censorship, an escalation of conservative rhetoric and a crackdown on activists halted this trend. In the U.S. cities where black and hispanic poverty brings to mind the hardships of apartheid, there is unfocused discontent. Elsewhere there is complacency or quietude, although on the U.S. campuses in the late 1980s, evidence exists of renewed concern for social justice.

Economic sanctions have hurt the racist regime in South Africa. The campaign to stop oil to South Africa and to boycott Shell have been especially costly. If the campaign to break ties with apartheid is to grow, more emphasis needs to be given to education and the power of the personal boycott. We each need to find out which corporations support apartheid, such as Coca-Cola, and refuse to purchase anything associated with that name. Pass it on, tell people about what you are doing and why and encourage them to do the same. Write letters to such corporations and let them know that you don't support them. The personal is political.

1. Brian Bunting notes the first use of the term "apartheid" by "Die Burger" on March 26, 1943. "The Origins of Apartheid", in Alex La Guma, "Apartheid" (New York: International Publishers, 1971), p.23. Cited in *Anti-Apartheid.*

Other references:

Reagan, Ronald, *"Sanctions are Immoral"* speech made July 22, 1986. cited by; Mermelstein, David, ed., in *The Anti-Apartheid Reader: The Struggle Against White Racist Rule in South Africa.* (New York: Grove Press, 1987), p. 516.

Love, Janice. *The U.S. Anti-Apartheid Movement: Local Activism in Global Politics.* (New York: Praeger Publishers, 1985), p.33.

Women in Southern Africa doing needlework for sale: Gabarone, tswana, 1987

Photographer: Terisa Turner

115

The U.S.A. at War

Infiltration of foreign economies with American-style consumerism and worship of American products

Bombardment at home with endless commercial products (Americans are "free" to onsume...and be consumed)

Propaganda at home is often disguised as entertainment. Sensational headlines and the high-tech culture of imperialism aim to induce paranoia and a war psychosis.

Propaganda at home is often disguised as entertainment. Sensational headlines and the high-tech culture of imperialism aim to induce paranoia and a war psychosis.

Illegal invasions, destruction of homes and relocation of people (Grenada, Lebanon, Central America)

Illegal evictions, arson, displacement and relocation of people (Harlem, Park Slope, Lower East Side)

Economic support for racist countries: In South Africa, the majority black population must, by law, carry pass books at all times. The USA, SA's #1 business partner, is currently investing over 2.3 billion dollars directly.

Protection for and collaboration with the Ku Klux Klan, Nazis, Lyndon LaRouche and other right-wing terrorist groups.

Nov. 6, 1976: The N.Y. Times reported that South African police have benefited by their relations with the USA — studying US riot control methods.

The Central Intelligence Agency "gathers information" overseas--originally barred from domestic spying on U.S. citizens....

The Federal Bureau of Information gathers information in this country--. involved in political surveillance, harassment and counter-insurgency...

Dec: 4, 1981: President Reagan signs order allowing the "...CIA to engage in domestic counter intelligence in cooperation with the FBI..."

The Military

The Police

Chemical Warfare

Nerve Gas, Napalm, Agent Orange, etc.

Drug Warfare

Alcohol, Heroin, Cocaine, Paraquat...

Overseas intervention, bombing, imprisonment and genocide of indigenous populations....

At home people are pitted against each other by a parasitic ruling class founded on slavery and stolen land.

Why Men Need To Be Pro-Feminist

Timothy A. Belknap

I thought I understood *how things worked*, and I was pessimistic. Now I think I understand *how things work*, and I am optimistic about our new world. I like to consider myself a regular male and a pro-feminist.

Uprising

Listen! There is something going on all over the universe that is going to drastically change **your** life within the next decade. People of all genders, races, and classes are no longer allowing themselves to be ruthlessly exploited. They know, and they are rising. One consolidated movement against sexism, racism, and classism, that's what we've got. You are already involved, there's no escaping that. This combined struggle surges ahead whether you are ready for it or not. Capitalism, the perpetrator of everyone's grief, will not survive.

Everyone feels the grief, especially the people that are challenged by the multiple injustices inflicted by sexism, racism, and classism. The worst hit are poverty stricken women of color. They know it, and they are rising against it.

A feminist is someone who admits that women are exploited and who fights to end that exploitation. Feminism can bring about mutual trust and obligation between the sexes. The power of feminism will dictate change in **everyone's** life and destiny within the next decade. That is why **every** male needs to get his shit together, now. It doesn't matter which race, class, or sexual orientation you've got. Women won't take **any** bullshit from anyone! Get hip to the progress of women. Support women who take charge of their own destinies. This will not only veer you away from a corrupt, fruitless life, but might actually save your life.

Read Calvin C. Hernton's **The Sexual Mountain and Black Women Writers** (all books I mention are listed at the end). It's a first-rate book. Calvin Hernton; a woman-conscious, woman-identified, black male; *knows where it's at*. He writes that our eyes must "be opened to the realities of women's lives and women's feelings and the realities of all our feelings and lives, in ways we are thoroughly trained to deny and ignore." [156] Everyone must see through the false realities imposed by capitalism.

Reject capitalism in all of its forms. Capitalism's program of brainwashing has instilled fear of deviation in each and everyone of us. People are scared. And most people find it convenient to hide behind words and models that expose as little truth, and thus emotion, as possible. There is a high concentration of these people where it matters the most: in universities and colleges. These people are 'bourgeois social scientists' who practice deceptions like making 'models' or using cheap, unprovoking words and make a profit doing it.

The typical things bourgeois social scientists do include using words like 'oppression', which are extremely intangible. What exactly is someone doing when they 'oppress' another person? Nobody can tell. It is quite vague. Now, if we substitute the word 'exploitation' for oppression amazing things happen. 'Exploitation' is much more concrete and actually holds some emotion. You can just picture some ass stealing a streetperson's last can of beans. Come on now, people don't go around oppressing people. They exploit them.

Bourgeois social scientists also hide behind models and theories. No branch of science is innocent, since useless theories and models are presented in all of them. Most of the models are just cheap substitutions for the truth. They involve useless circles of thought that divert and lead people away from the reality of exploitation. From neo-classical economics to psychoanalytic theory, (complete with penis envy!) all social sciences sport mainstream practitioners who cover-up the exploitation of others. And the thing is academics try to push these silly models on **us** so that **they** can make a living. These people are killing us to make a buck. 'Making a buck' is a disease that has infiltrated all areas of society. Especially diseased are the areas where social change should be implemented. Feminism is no exception.

Sexual Objectifiers

John Stoltenberg, a writer on male-female relations, knows that people would rather hide behind words and models than discover the truth. He writes that "it is the fashion to describe human conduct in language that obscures the fact of acts, and the fact that acts have consequences, and the fact that one is connected to one's acts whether or not one is 'in touch' with them. It is also the fashion to call acts 'reactions', as if the agent really responsible for the act were someone or something else." [p.5] Men are especially guilty of this in their relations with women. Men find out that it is easier and much more convenient to hide behind words than to face-up to reality. Or if a man strikes a woman then he will blame it on "losing his head", or something else equally unacceptable. Stoltenberg points this out in his writing about sexual objectification.

Sexual objectification is the process in which one person makes another out to be an object that can be easily, unemotionally fucked. When a man needs to make a woman out to be an object, in order to "have sex" with her, he must also remove himself from the reality of exploiting her for her service. The man can't even try to apply ethics to his actions because it is too deeply disturbing.

The points that John Stoltenberg bring up are extremely important, especially to the male who aspires to support feminist concerns. Every male has had to be a sexual objectifier in order to validate his masculinity "trip". In our capitalistic society, it is mandatory that every male has to sexually violate a woman in order to become a "real man". If he refuses to violate a woman then he is seen as a homosexual.

Homosexuality and Power

Homosexuality is a tremendous threat to the hierarchy of power under capitalism. The United States military is a prime example of this. As if in a craze, the military screens their enlistments heavily in order to weed out the homosexuals. Why is this? They are scared shitless because homosexuality has the potential to undermine hierarchies of power. How can you kill or command men you may love? Also, homosexuality is surrounded by a group of false theories. These theories attempt to justify discrimination against and exploitation of homosexuals. We need 'real men' to fight and it is possible that the military brass think that some sort of "lack of masculinity" will spread like a disease through their ranks!

Female homosexuality is a tremendous threat to the system. Men need to violate women in order to be "real men" in this society. What would happen if all women decided to ignore men or just be separatists? Men would be disturbed, since the exploitation of women is such an integral part of the power hierarchy.

Let's go back to the hierarchy of power. Joseph Pleck describes why men feel a need to exploit women. Unfortunately Pleck gets highly psychological when he does this. He insists that men see women as holding some sort of powers over them, which supposedly explains why men find a need to exploit women.

Pleck's psychological analysis starts out by attributing two main powers that men might *see* women as having over them. Traditionally, he says, women expressed emotions for men. They also made men feel masculine. Pleck argues that men fear that women will no longer do these things for them. This psychological approach is objectionable because it suggests that everything will be OK if this fear which men harbor can be eased or overcome. Contrast this to Hernton's approach that only with total transformation of the capitalist, sexist, racist social order will everything be OK.

Pleck continues on his quest for psychological comfort. He goes on to explain that men "use" women in the following ways: (1)as symbols of success, (2)in mediating roles between males, (3)as refuges from the dangers and stresses of a man's world, and (4)as an underclass in man's society. Pleck might be touching on facts here, but like many facts, these points obscure the truth, because they are limited to the realm of psychology. A material and historical analysis is needed. We want to know why men use women in these ways. Then the solution would not be sought at the level of psychology: men getting rid of bad ideas and replacing them with good ones. This naive and untruthful approach would have to make way for a revolutionary re-ordering of society, worldwide, to get rid of exploitation in all its forms.

Pleck's analysis is clinical. It's sterile and unemotional, and therefore it is as far from reality as possible. **Real** actions have **real** consequences for **real** people. People have often failed to point this out, and consequently, theorized movements out of existence. That is why men must realize their position in relation to the women's movement and feminism.

Men can take strong stands against sexism and heterosexism (a belief in the superiority of heterosexual over homosexual relations) amongst themselves. There is plenty for males to do amongst themselves. There is no need for them to intervene in the women's movement. The women's movement needs its autonomy to split from the rotten male ways that have dominated over them for so long. Men are also sly dogs: they have excelled in cheating on, domineering over, and competing for women for too many years.

Men can actually compete at who is being most cooperative with women. Most can be quite successful doing this, too. Through even very minimal cooperation with women, men can easily attain the status of 'special male'. 'Special males' get special attention, such as gaining undeserved access to women, and undeserved ethical acknowledgement by all. There is no room nor time in the women's movement for such superficiality. No men should even try to intrude into the women's movement because it would, in itself, be a violation of women's autonomy.

There are unlimited ways for men of serious, good intentions to work for the equality of women. Men must confront other men about women's exploitation, including violence against women: especially battering of women, incest, rape, and pornography. Men must also confront heterosexism and homophobia in other men. The consequences of these actions will be the pioneering of new social relations between the sexes.

Men who **now** support women who are taking charge of their lives will be a thousand times better off. They will lead lives that are filled with true equality, democracy and thus, happiness.

Books reflected in the text:

Hernton, Calvin C.; *The Sexual Mountain and Black Women Writers*; Anchor Press, New York, NY; 1987.

Pleck, Elizabeth H., and Joseph H. Pleck, *The American Man*; Prentice-Hall, Inc., Englewood Cliffs, NJ; 1974.

Pleck, Joseph H., and Jack Sawyer, *Men and Masculinity*; Prentice-Hall, Inc., Englewood Cliffs, NJ; 1974.

Rich, Adrienne; "Compulsory Heterosexuality and Lesbian Existence"; *Signs: A Journal of Women in Culture and Society*; May 4, 1980.

Baumli, Francis, ed.; *Men Freeing Men, Exploding the Myth of the Traditional Male*; New Atlas Press, Jersey City, NJ; 1985.

Bianchi, Eugene C.; "The Superbowl Culture of Male Violence"; *The Christian Century*; September 18,1974;p.842-845.

Brod, Harry, ed.; *The Making of Masculinities, The New Men's Studies*; Allen & Unwin, Inc., Boston, MA; 1987.

"Men and Friendship: Noble Companions or Companionable Competitors?" *Friendship*, p.53-77.

Stoltenberg, John; *Disarmament and Masculinity*; Frog in the Well Publishing, Palo Alto, CA; 1978.

Stoltenberg, John; "Men's Pornography, Men's Selves"; 1981,1982; *Sourjourner*; May 1982.

Linoleum cut of Langston Hughes by Rachael Romero, 1983.

Langston Hughes was a woman-identified poet.

127

CAN YOU RECOGNIZE A TERRORIST?

KNOW THE DIFFERENCES BETWEEN:

 A TERRORIST, and... A FREEDOM-FIGHTER

 HOSTAGES, and... POLITICAL PRISONERS

 BOMBING AN EMBASSY, and... MINING A FOREIGN HARBOR

 NATIONALIST FANATICS, and... PATRIOTIC CITIZENS

DO YOU ACTUALLY BELIEVE
WHAT GOVERNMENT OFFICIALS SAY?

DONNELLY COLT CUSTOM PRINTING BOX 188 HAMPTON CONN 06247

Love, Politics and Escape From the U.S. Air Force

Ralph Reed

I guess I want to tell you about the period in my life when I flirted with fame, when power stirred from its uneasy slumber and threatened to crash into my bedroom. It was a time when I hoped for glory. But I fell apart, and my lover, upon whose shoulders the burden of our acts was squarely placed, proved to be the one who was strong and heroic.

I joined the Air Force two days after the Christmas of 1983, a fucked-up 19 year old looking for a way out. The four years before this last desperate act were filled with expulsions: from prep school, my father's house, hick high school number one, my mother's house, hick high school number two, drug rehab, my mother's house again, and finally my dad's house. I was sick of not belonging. The military appealed to me as a purgatory, a place where I could cleanse my soul before society applied its own cleansers in the form of state homes and prisons. Something big out there didn't like me, and I needed to act fast before my life got totally trashed.

I was relieved to have the Air Force make my decisions for me. They flew me from my small town home in Maine to Texas for basic training, where I found their attempts at brainwashing me superficial, if a bit surreal. Many of my comrades seemed to succumb which frightened and alienated me. But the consequences of reacting in my usual way to this fear and alienation were all too apparent, and so my behavior was modified, even if my internal world continued to spin contrary to the dictates of flag and country. I'd played the games of prison-like institutions before, only I'd always chosen to lose; this time the stakes were higher: I played to survive.

After a month of basic, I was shipped off to technical school in Biloxi, Mississippi, where I spent five alcohol-sodden weeks learning how to be a computer operator. The Air Force started to paint me as undesirable, thanks to several "alcohol-related incidents" (the bureaucracy's term for diving off the stage at the Airmen's Club and telling the Security Police that I was a communist terrorist for Castro). A psychiatrist told my commander that I was "extremely intelligent, nonconformist, covert, and narcissistic," but not "alcoholic," so I managed to push on to my first and last assignment in the "real" Air Force--Space Command's 1000th Satellite Operations Group at Offutt Air Force Base in Omaha, Nebraska.

My life shattered as I arrived in Omaha. On a 30 hour bus ride from Biloxi I had bought 15 hits of LSD and a Talking Heads tape from a musician who claimed to be Ken Kesey's nephew. The acid over-powered me and a couple of others who took it, causing us to be searched by a sheriff when we arrived in Omaha. I ate the 12 remaining hits, in order to avoid a term at Fort Leavenworth (the Federal Penitentiary for military personnel), and holed-up in a fleabag hotel downtown, having the deepest and longest psychotic break of my life.

I made it out to the Air Force Base a day late, broke and feeling broken. I was introduced to the computer room and the people who worked there, and proceeded to drink two month's pay in the next month. One night, during my ritual of post-club puking, I had somewhat of an awakening, and found myself the next day going through withdrawal at an AA meeting. The following two months saw me get my act together enough to participate in the real drama I want to tell you about, the story of my relationship with Jesus (not his real name) and its dissolution.

When I was two months sober, I fell in love with Jesus. I met him in the barracks one night as I was shooting pool and hoping someone would notice me. He seemed appreciative, and somehow magically other, like me. I liked the acceptance I saw in his eyes, and he made me feel like I could be myself. I had always been "straight," but when he told me he was gay I told him that I might like to be too. We started making love in an Air Force housing development, at a house that Jesus was watching for a friend. The Los Angeles Olympics were on TV, and we fought over whether the patriotism was a good thing. Jesus was a Mexican-American from Texas, who was becoming conservative after a liberal past. I agreed with him on so many levels, I couldn't understand why he should be reactionary in this one regard. Later I would comprehend, when he shared the awful secret of his work.

After a couple of weeks Jesus' friend returned, so we moved our affair into the barracks. Jesus' roommate had moved off base, but even so, we had to be careful we weren't discovered. Sometimes a knock came, and I would leap up naked and dart behind the shower curtain before Jesus opened the door to receive his guest. The bigger, potentially dangerous world conflicted with our intimate, secret life, so we shut it out as best as we could, trying to create a space where we could be safe.

One night, while we made the darkness our own as we lay together on our tiny bed, Jesus told me about his job. He began by saying he shouldn't tell me, that it was "top secret;" but that he felt he must share it with me. He told me that he was a spy, a "Spanish cryptologic linguist," who flew over Central America and the Caribbean eavesdropping. He said that he felt that he was betraying his people by doing it, but that he thought perhaps the job was necessary. In any case he was trapped; they wanted him to do his job.

As I listened to him I felt a sense of drama, as if our private world was growing larger. Part of me felt moral outrage, horror; another part felt complicit and hypocritical; and the most significant part of me felt overwhelmingly worried--the feeling you get when a child walks too close to the edge of a cliff. We both seemed like children to me, stuck in adult roles that threatened to make us into monsters.

I began to feel like a "good Nazi," surrounded by "bad Nazis" in a Nazi system. I was worse than them, I thought, because I was aware that our acts were in an important sense criminal, yet did nothing. Jesus, though his hands were bloodier than mine, was forced to rationalize it away in order to live with himself. I found my own way of explaining things and protecting us: I tried to find out the faults of the world that made us sinners. We moved out of the barracks to an apartment in Omaha. I started to get magazines. My choices were progressively more radical, as I subscribed to every offer that came to our place in the mail. We joined a natural food co-op, and ended up associated with a group of radicals we could be "out" with. Jesus tried to hide his job from everyone, while I kept blurting it out. I wanted to connect the facts of our lives; Jesus needed to keep them separate.

We dreamed of the day we would both be out of the Air Force. We would move to Maine, where I had brought Jesus a couple of times to meet my family and experience my favorite habitats. There we would help each other finish college and become teachers. We would live close to the land, have many colorful friends, and be free.

Though our lives seemed to be growing more open and pleasant, there was a dark side that kept asserting itself. At least two nights a week, Jesus would don his flight suit at 2 o'clock in the morning, and carry his gear off to the base. He would attend a 3 o'clock briefing, then at dawn the plane would head South. He would return in the evening smelling of sweat and looking exhausted. He had enlisted for six years, and had three to go. He was in danger of being transferred to Panama, where there were ground stations and another air base. If he tried to cross-train into another job, we would probably be separated when he was assigned overseas. While the Air Force tried to keep married couples together, they hadn't a policy for keeping fags happy.

Worse, Jesus was breaking down under the stress of his job. He asked me which bone he should break in order to be taken off "flight status." One night we went to an all night drug store to purchase a syrup that causes vomiting. He packed it in his lunch and drank some as his crew was getting briefed. His gambit worked, but he came home at 4 o'clock in the morning feeling ill. Nightmares began haunting him, and he would wake up screaming and shaking almost every night.

The fear was killing me too. I hated for him to leave and while he was gone I worried about him. What if his plane crashed, or was shot down? The United States was preparing for war with Nicaragua, and I thought that a "Sandinista provocation" like the shooting down of an American plane over Honduran soil was perfect pretext for invasion. I started trying to get Jesus to read accounts of the Contra War, but he couldn't stand to and would become infuriated with me for badgering him. He said that his work harmed nobody because they were incompetent and by the time the tapes were translated the battles had moved elsewhere.

But then he met Antonio. Some of our friends were Sanctuary workers and knew Jesus spoke Spanish. They wished him to translate for a Salvadoran refugee who they'd bailed out of a federal holding pen in Louisiana. Jesus agreed to translate, and they became friends. Antonio told Jesus about El Salvador; about the 14 family members and friends who had been killed by death squads; and about the bombs and the terror. Jesus kept his job a secret from Antonio, but he was forced to confront the dreadful reality of his work.

Soon after meeting Antonio, Jesus was given a short term assignment to Panama. This we both had wanted to avoid. Separation for more than a few days had always been nearly unbearable, and months could pass while Jesus struggled to maintain his sanity in Panama without my support. I grew angry, and adamant that he must find a way out of his orders. But we found no way to escape the inexorable dictates of power, and so Jesus left, alone and afraid.

While in Panama, he decided to stop doing his job, one way or another. Upon his return, we started looking for the best way for him to wash his hands of it, without ending up in jail. I had become embittered by the stress and wanted him to go for the Air Force's jugular by a public disavowal. The Central American anti-intervention movement had succeeded in raising U.S. public consciousness about Washington's military policy to the extent that many people including those in the military no longer believed the rationale of the government. Contragate was in full swing and the time seemed right for attack. The battle over 'the hearts and minds' had become a great concern of the Pentagon, and they seemed certain to lose if Jesus went public with his job. Having prepared for the past four years to invade Nicaragua with regular U.S. troops, the military establishment was trying to gracefully withdraw from this posture with the unwanted scrutiny of the media and the Congress.

In Panama, Jesus had discovered that the radio data they caught in the air had been transmitted back to the Contras on the ground in 'real time' (at the same time). Because this was operating procedure during the time of the Boland Amendment (a congressional act limiting the role of the United States government in supporting the Contras) the Air Force was directly aiding the Contras in defiance of the law. In order to protect themselves, the 'spin control' of the intelligence bureaucracies on Contragate held that the law had been broken by a rogue element in the National Security Council. If Jesus were to go public with his job, he would help establish that in actuality the entire foreign policy apparatus of the United States government was complicit in breaking the law. It seemed to me that Jesus had a unique opportunity to confront the United States Empire with its own contradictions. Rather than meekly submit to its orders, he could condemn it, redeem himself and perhaps help the very people he had been hurting.

After the story of Jesus' refusal to continue in his job was leaked in the *U.S. Guardian* (New York) by his lawyers, all hell exploded. The *Omaha World Herald* received a tip from a local peace activist and the next day ran the story on the front page. In this story, Jesus was inaccurately quoted as saying that he had been flying military reconnaissance in direct support of the contras and the Salvadoran Guard during the period of the Boland Amendment. The military responded by going after Jesus' family, calling his Master Sergeant brother on to the carpet in order to find out what Jesus was up to. Meanwhile the San Antonio paper hounded his parents.

Jesus was horrified but also furious at his family being brought into the fray and decided to hold a press conference. His lawyers and the entire Omaha peace community held a rally in support of Jesus, and the next day at the Omaha Press Club, he appeared before the national media: CBS, AP, the Boston Globe, UPI and the local broadcast and print media. Jesus accused the airforce of intimidating him through his family while remaining close-mouthed about anything that could be construed as classified. However his lawyers were explicit about his role and said that Jesus would testify in further detail before a Congressional committee. That evening the local TV stations ran his testimony as the top story and CBS evening news counterpointed Oliver North's testimony with Jesus' story.

After this media onslaught, Jesus was a hero in the peace community but despised on the airforce base. While his conscientious objector status was being decided within the military judicial system; three separate investigations were launched by his military command at the Pentagon, the Air Force Office of Special Investigations (AFOSI), and most frighteningly, at the National Security Agency (NSA). NSA, the little-known agency, had become an integral part of the U.S intelligence bureaucracy, serving as the electronically oriented analog of the CIA. They had been the chief end users of the information collected by Jesus' spy flights. Their desire to remain hidden was the key that could free Jesus from his servitude.

Meanwhile, within Jesus' unit and Offutt Air Force Base, the military community was galvanized with the urge to persecute and ultimately prosecute him. "Treason" and "espionage" were his crimes, according to the majority popular and elite opinion. However, a considerable minority of those on the ground, particularly those who had a direct role in military intervention in the Third World (for instance, Vietnamese, Farsi and Arabic linguists along with their Spanish counterparts), covertly expressed their support and admiration for Jesus' decision and action. Some expressed the view that they would do the same thing if it weren't for the economic needs of their families. In my unit many of the airmen followed Jesus' case avidly, regarding him as a courageous local celebrity. Despite agonizing interrogations and sickening suspense, our plan worked. Though Jesus' command wanted to burn him at the stake for treason, the prudence of NSA and Pentagon's elite caused Jesus to be set free with an honorable discharge.

As Jesus confronted the Air Force, I deserted him. I had fallen in love with a woman. The pressure had proven too much for me, and I wished to escape it. Jesus had to endure the most difficult struggle of his life without me. I left him in his time of ultimate need, because I couldn't handle it, because my heart had gravitated toward another. He saw me fleeing my gayness for a socially sanctified domesticity, destroying the possibility of his dreams at the time he needed them most. I am only a human, weak and fragile, yet I pretended to be strong enough to carry us both. He seemed entirely dependent upon me, yet he proved heroic.

Ralph Reed received an honorable discharge from the U.S. Air Force in December 1987. He is currently living in Wendell, Massachusetts and pursuing a BA with a major in Social Thought and Political Theory at the University of Massachusetts in Amherst.

Male Total Destruct
Pencil drawing by Benjamin Bennett

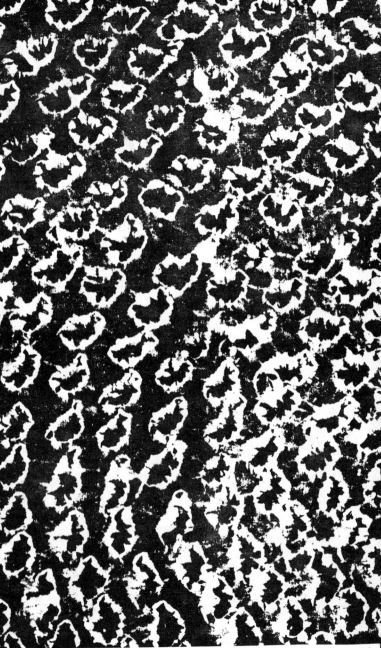

Photocopy of tie dyed wrap cloth made by Yoruba craftswoman in Ife, Nigeria, 1984

138

The Rainforest, The Dead and Digital: Using Worldwide Communications Networks To Encourage Planetary Survival

David Caputo

David Caputo is a 24 year old student, computer programmer and political activists who spent the first 18 years of his life in Peabody, Massachusetts. When not studying, programming and pursuing politics; he spends his time teaching therapeutic massage techniques, inventing board games and promoting musical groups. He also plays guitar and has a 92 average as a candlepin bowler. He has worked at Digital Equipment Corporation headoffice in Maynard, near Boston, off and on since 1984. The most intense experience in his life (so far) was attending a rally on June 12, 1982 in New York City where over one million (1,000,000) people showed up to protect the earth from Reagan's proposed 'winnable' nuclear war. This gave him hope that the human race was indeed interested in propagating itself and protecting our habitat, Earth.

Introduction
Inside the company

In North America, the world is a very strange place. Much of the world's wealth is concentrated here. The hard work of our forebearers from Europe and Africa is piled up in communities like Weston, Massachusetts, Greenwich, Connecticut and Washington DC. One part of that affluent subculture is the international colossus known as Digital Equipment Corporation. Digital, or DEC for short, employs approx 100,000 people worldwide. Everywhere there is a Digital computer, there is at least a field service office to fix it if it breaks down. All (or most) of these people have access to a terminal and a computer. All (or most) of the computers are linked together in a worldwide communication network. At last count there were over 30,000 computers, or "nodes", in DEC's Easynet (tm) internal network. This makes it the largest private non-military computer network in the world.

Employees at Digital have access to a vast repertoire of software tools: editors, graphics packages, electronic mail, VAXphone (similar to a Teletype), all computer languages, and much more. These tools, and one other called NOTES that I will describe in more detail later, constitute a powerful resource with which to discover, communicate, and debate information about the world. The size and scope of this network, and others like it, provide historically unprecedented communication ability. This phenomenon is central to the question of revolutionary popular culture, both because of its implications for revolutionary movements in USA client states (and elsewhere), and for its impact and usefulness in modern USA culture.

The Grateful Dead

The Grateful Dead are two things: a rock band and a subculture. The band is very good. Its musicians play many concerts each year and have been doing so with amazing consistency for about 23 years. The subculture is an interesting blend of old hippies, new hippies, high school kids, high school dropouts, drifters, young parents, older parents (both with kids), and various other individualistic types. Members of this subculture are sometimes called Dead Heads. They take pride in a sense of comradeship and sister/brotherhood. The Grateful Dead allow members of the audience to audio tape the live concerts, so there is a huge collection of live concert tapes which are traded within the Dead Head clan. It is a motorized, nomadic culture. Singing, dancing, smoking, tripping,love, colors, travel, beauty, music and laughter make up its tapestries.

Here people largely reject the dog-eat-dog competition that makes up the corporobureaucratic professional world. Many Dead Heads come from the middle class, and have been groomed to enter it all their lives. Those who follow the Dead are seeking something other than what official society has planned for them. This search for an alternative to the corporate definition of life charges the Dead Head movement with revolutionary cultural potential.

I traveled this summer to Tacoma, Washington; Eugene, Oregon; Landover,Maryland and New York City to see a total of seven

Child in tee-short of U.S. flag at Grateful Dead concert in Oregon, 1988
Photographer: David Caputo

Grateful Dead shows. The Dead were accompanied in these shows by Santana.

in Tacoma and Jimmy Cliff and Robert Cray in Eugene, making the experience somewhat multi-cultural. My companion Mike and I kept a log book and asked people to write down their thoughts about popular revolutionary culture as it relates to the Grateful Dead. We got many brilliant responses: poems, artwork, essays, addresses. Unfortunately, a mix-up resulted in the book being left in someone's car who drove off to North Carolina with it. We did take photographs however, and reproduce some of them here.

The Rainforest

The rainforest ties everything together. Well almost. Let me explain. Only a small portion of the land area on the surface of the earth is what biologists call "rainforest". However, these areas generate a full forty percent (40%) of the world's oxygen supply. Without oxygen, we die in three to five (3-5) minutes so there is a common interest here. There is also the issue of species. The rainforests are a treasure trove of life. Thousands of animals and plants from those regions have never been recorded by USA scientists. They are being wiped out before we even know they exist. Global rainforest biomass is being permanently destroyed at a staggering rate. In June, July, and August of 1988, a land area nine (9) times the size of Massachusetts burned in Brazil alone! The greenhouse effect is rapidly accelerated by this type of action. The burning releases carbon dioxide (CO_2) into the atmosphere. Healthy trees hold it in their lush canopy. Trees actually "eat" carbon dioxide, turning it into oxygen, reducing its accumulation in the atmosphere.

The burning is being done to "clear the land" for "development". This usually means cattle ranching, or plantation farming. Formerly landless city dwellers may be sent into the jungle on some government or World Bank - financed "trans-migration" program to get them out of the cities. In the cities, the poor can organize and take control of their lives, like they do in Peru. These "rural development" programs are fraudulent rip-offs.

The cattle ranching is one of the worst ideas. The land is "cleared" and grass or alfalfa is planted. Then cows are brought in to eat the grass and get fat. In the process their hooves churn up the ground, disturbing further a soil shocked from burning and clearing. This, and the invariably thin character of all rainforest soils, combine with the rains to wash away all the topsoil in one to five (1-5) years. Then the land is useless desert, a mockery of the lush forests that once stood. The pattern has already been made clear. Disappearing forest leads to a change in weather patterns, bringing droughts to what was once constantly wet. The way the ranchers get the land is evil too. The government - financed "pioneer" programs I just mentioned get city poor to clear land once covered in jungle. The land is then taken from them at gunpoint by the agents of the ranchers. The "pioneers" get a choice: flee to forested lands and clear them, or be killed in their homes. See the article about "Chico" Mendez in appendix D.

Plantation farming is just as bad, devastating huge tracts of land, forcing workers to slave for a pittance or face the discipline of starvation. The land-owning corporate farmers lash out at all who would seek to stop the destruction or redistribute the benefits. The environmental damage is acute, from clearing and burning and from the impact of worker communities brought in to previously virgin lands. The large scale monocropping leads to high applications of poisonous chemicals for pests previously kept in check by nature. I stand mute with horror at times just contemplating the savagery and calculated planning that goes into this systematic attack on our life-support system. How could someone advocate capital punishment for a murderer, while the men who destroy so much are 'respectable businessmen'in USA society? The banality of evil which Hannah Arendt said characterized Nazi war crimes is still very much with us.

Network For Survival

What do Digital, the Dead and the rainforests have in common? For one thing, I work at Digital, tour with the Dead, and agitate to preserve the rainforest. This links them in my mind. They are also linked by an activity that I am participating in to stop a stupid and irresponsible initiative on the part of the World Bank.

There is a loan, the Power Sector II loan to Brazil, which includes a five hundred million dollar ($500,000,000.00) project to build the Kararoa Dam on the Xingu River as part of the Altimara Hydropower Project. This is an unbelievably bad idea. Huge dam loans to Brazil have caused catastrophic ecological damage to large areas of the country. The rising effects of the buildup of greenhouse gases in the atmosphere is partially a result of these loans. The increased urbanization of previously undamaged rainforest creates further damage causing an environmental ripple effect which wipes out a tremendous amount of life. Not only is local animal and plant life destroyed or forced to flee, but indigenous civilizations which had previously lived in harmony with their surroundings are uprooted and either killed outright, forced to work to death on the project, or displaced into refugee camps and squatter villages, constantly in fear of the army.

One such incident, as relayed to me by Francis Moore Lappe, author of *Diet for a Small Planet* and *A Fate Worse Than Debt*, is about a two billion dollar ($2,000,000,000.00) dam project. It seems that corporate executives did not want to go to the expense of cutting down the timber in the vast region that was to be flooded. So, they cut down about three percent of it (3%) and hired a company from the USA to get rid of the rest. The company got hold of some old surplus USA army Agent Orange, and sprayed it all over this beautiful, life filled, forest. The area was subsequently flooded and is now the primary water source for a city of one million (1,000,000) people who were drawn to this once sparsely populated area to, what else, work on the dam. This sad tale does not end here. There are several barrels of Agent Orange which are missing and presumed to be mired somewhere at the bottom of the lake. Should they burst near any of the water supply inflow pipes...

The dam itself, built to provide electricity to Brazil's cities and industry, is now useless, choked with silt from the runoff of denuded hillsides. Poverty, misery, and despair are the norm out here. One would hope that human race, or at least the venture capitalists at the World Bank, would learn from obvious, glaring, mistakes. But no, they now propose the Kararoa Dam, to build another wasteful, destructive, and ultimately useless monument to the wasteful arrogance of some men. It is sickening. That is why I am resisting it.

Rainforest Action Network is a grass-roots information exchange system. Local groups from around the country work on mobilizing public opinion on rainforest issues. A national office keeps tabs on developments in Washington, D.C. with help from concerned citizens from all over the world who call and write with rainforest news. These groups are networked through newsletters, action campaigns, and telephone trees. The aim of the organization is to get as much information out to as many people as possible.

The Grateful Dead recently issued "An Appeal to Reason from the Grateful Dead" concerning the rainforest. This brought the issue before thousands of people, including the attenders at a benefit concert for Greenpeace at Madison Square Garden this fall.

Debating on the Electronic Bulletin Board

The Grateful Dead is also the title of a Digital NOTES file that I have access to every working day. A notes file is an electronic bulletin board on which people can write messages and respond to other messages left by others on the system. A dialog can be set up on virtually any topic. As the rainforest issue has been embraced by the Grateful Dead, the Dead NOTES file is an excellent place to communicate information on that subject. There is another notes file called Environmental Issues and I have used it to communicate rainforest information as well. I typed up a broadsheet (see Appendix A) and entered it into the two previously mentioned NOTES files and the History and Defense Issues NOTES files. The reaction from the Defense Issues NOTES was sudden. "Give me one good reason why I should not erase this right away," said the NOTES file moderator. I gave several, (see Appendix B) and the moderator acquiesced to the presence of my message on the system. However, several noters in the Defense Issues file objected to its presence and it was subsequently removed.

The response from the other NOTES files was much more positive (see Appendix C). Several people wrote in to encourage others to participate. Many of them posted the letters that they had written so that they could be used as prototypes for those who were having difficulty composing a letter on their own. Many were outraged by the

In every Central American country the production of meat has skyrocketed. At times it seems that the isthmus is on the way to becoming one great stock ranch. Twenty years ago the Pan American highway passed through extensive tracts of tropical forest. Today its entire paved length is through cropland and planted pasture.

It is a myth that rain forest soil is rich. The ecosystem of the rain forest is a closed one in which the nutrients are to be found in the living canopy of plants and in the thin layer of humus on the ground that is formed from the matter shed by the canopy.

What happens when the big cattle ranchers level a few tens of thousands of acres of tropical forest? For the first few years the soil grows well thriving on the former biomass. After that the soil becomes exposed and the area becomes useless for agriculture.

...since much of the land now being used for pasture is the most fertile available, food crop production is increasingly being relegated to more marginal land. In addition, a large proportion of the grains that are produced are now fed to livestock.

Thus the ultimate beneficiaries of the conversion of land from forests and grain crop production in Central America are the land owners, the corporations that control the meat processing plants, and ultimately the people of the United States and their pets.

TWO DOUBLE BACON BURGERS PLEASE!

Don't worry it all goes into the same belly.

Text from The Political Economy of Deforestation by Kathy DeWalt published in The Bulletin of Atomic Scientists ... ... 1984. Also thanks to: Swamp Thing The Curse and DC Comics, with J. Miller

information I presented them and vowed to give their sincere attention to the issue both now and in the future.

The Rainforest Action Network does an excellent job using communication networks to encourage planetary survival. They regularly send out letters to all the people on their worldwide mailing list, informing them of pressing issues and attempting to motivate action on specific World Bank loans and other environmental issues. This direct mail campaign is supported and augmented by use of other communication networks. Local Rainforest Action groups have 'telephone trees' to spread information throughout the local area. Individuals in the groups call other people who have expressed interest in these issues and inform them of the latest developments. These people, in turn, are encouraged to call friends and family and spread the word even further. In addition to calling friends and family, people do other work to spread the word. This work includes putting up posters, demonstrating, honoring boycotts, writing letters to the editor, and posting notes in electronic bulletin boards such as the one I described earlier.

The People Have the Power

One excellent example of this type of information distribution is the successful boycott and publicity campaign waged against Burger King and its parent corporation, Pillsbury. Burger King was one of the world's largest purchasers of rainforest beef. They were singlehandedly responsible for the destruction of vast areas of tropical vegetation. Communication of this fact led to a boycott of Burger King and other Pillsbury products, and demonstrations at Burger King's across the USA. The corporation finally threw in the towel and cancelled huge contracts for Central American rainforest beef. This single event saved huge areas of forest which had been slated for development by ranchers under contract to Burger King. The negative publicity was too much for the King to handle.

All over the world, people are beginning to stare our impending ecological crisis in the face. From *Time* magazine, which recently named Earth "Planet of the Year", to the tree-hugging women of the "Chipko" movement in India, a cross-cultural and in many cases multi-class alliance is forming to defend life and protect our fragile home. No profits will be made on a cold, dead, world. No children will be raised, no symphonies composed, no races run, no homes built, no stocks traded, no baths taken, no voices heard. That is why we must hear YOUR voice today! As Star Trek's Chief Engineer Scott once said aboard the star ship Enterprise, "Captain, she can't take it much longer, we only have a few hours of life support left!"

Use the communication networks you have at your disposal. Talk to your friends, your family, your neighbors, your co-workers. Watch, read, and listen to the problems we face. Work with others to find creative solutions. Every human being has a duty to do what s/he can in order to preserve life for themselves and others. I want to be an ancestor. Our mother planet has given us life. Our life has given us thought. Our thoughts give us the ability to act. We must act now, act decisively, and take control over the decisions which threaten to destroy our home, planet Earth.

Appendix A

Alert! Alert! Alert!

Save the rainforest --- Save the rainforest

Call to all concerned inhabitants of planet earth: As you may know, the world's tropical rainforests are being destroyed at a catastrophic rate. This summer alone, in Brazil alone, 77,000 square miles of rainforest were observed burning by LANDSAT and other satellites. By way of comparison, Massachusetts is just over 8,000 square miles in size. This burning alone was responsible for 10% of ALL carbon dioxide pollution added to the atmosphere this year, rapidly accelerating the greenhouse effect. The WORLD BANK has had a big hand in funding this and other types of rainforest destruction, with devastating consequences for both the environment and the indigenous Indian tribes who had previously lived in harmony with their bountiful but fragile jungle. NOW, the WORLD BANK wants to loan Brazil $500,000,000.00 (that's FIVE HUNDRED MILLION DOLLARS) so that Brazil can CONTINUE TO DESTROY THE RAINFORESTS by BUILDING A HUGE DAM!!! The history of dam loans to Brazil is an ecological and economic nightmare. This loan is part of the POWER SECTOR II LOAN and the part specifically objected to is the ALTIMARA HYDRO project for the KARAROA DAM on the XINGU RIVER (pronounced zing-oo).Not only would this project FLOOD 866 SQUARE MILES OF PRISTINE RAINFOREST but it would also PERMANENTLY DESTROY TWO INDIGENOUS Indian TRIBES!!! This disruption of these indigenous tribes causes the loan to VIOLATE THE WORLD BANK'S OWN ENVIRONMENTAL CRITERIA!!! WE MUST OBJECT AND OBJECT LOUDLY!!!! The Indians who live in the area sent their two leaders KUBEI & PAYAKAN to Washington DC to speak with BARBAR CONABLE, the PRESIDENT OF THE WORLD BANK. Upon return to Brazil they were ARRESTED AND ARE CURRENTLY BEING HELD WITHOUT BAIL AS "FOREIGNERS INTERFERING WITH BRAZIL'S INTERNAL AFFAIRS". THEY ARE NOT EVEN RECOGNIZED AS CITIZENS OF BRAZIL EVEN THOUGH THEY LIVE THERE!!!!! This message is being relayed by thousands of people throughout the world right now and it affords a perfect opportunity to press for justice and preservation of our fragile planet. CALL BARBAR CONABLE!!! Tell him to cancel the POWER SECTOR II LOAN to Brazil. Better yet, WRITE TO HIM!!! No positive change has ever been caused except by grass roots pressure on those who make the decisions. We can change the course of human events. We CAN prevent this stupid and destructive loan from taking place. Post this notice, tell your friends, talk about it over dinner, we only have until DECEMBER 12, 1988. That is the day of the WORLD BANK VOTES on this loan. We can notify many people by then, especially if everyone tells their friends, who then tell their friends, and so on, and so on...

PLEASE HELP! KUBEI, PAYAKAN, AND MOTHER EARTH WILL THANK YOU!!
Call or write:
BARBAR CONABLE
WORLD BANK
1818 H St. S.W.
Washington,DC 20433
(202) 477-1234

Appendix B

Letter to moderator of Defence Issues NOTES file, Digital:

Dear Moderator,
I wish to apologize in advance for any trouble this may cause you. I am
new to this notesfile stuff and I am trying not to step out of bounds.
Please bear with me...

I have several reasons to believe that DEFENSE-ISSUES is an
appropriate forum for the note about the WORLD BANK AND
RAINFOREST DESTRUCTION.

1. This forum attracts intelligent people who have a concern about
issues involving global importance and large sums of money.

2. The US military apparatus (including the CIA) has had a big
hand in the establishment of political/economic order in BRAZIL that
supports this type of vastly destructive and wasteful project.

3. The arrogance and insensitivity to the lives of the local Indians
demonstrates a colonial/imperialist attitude that has long been a focus
of US military policy and should be critically examined.

4. The Brazilian military (financed and trained by the US for many
years) will actually be involved in violently suppressing local resistance
to this destructive project. This is evidenced by the imprisonment (in
military jails) of the two Indian leaders.

5. The devastating destruction of the rainforest is leading to
economic and social upheavals which may require US troops or
military aid to suppress. Also, in Central America, destruction of the
environment is a major factor in illegal immigration to the US, which
some people suggest the military should be involved in stopping.

6. Finally, there is the question of what is it that our military is
defending us from. A planet with its oxygen producing capacity
destroyed (the rainforest produces over 40% of the world's oxygen
supply) will be "defendable" by no amount of military firepower.

Also, I believe it is important to have a global perspective when considering military matters. The Soviet Union could destroy the United States simply by blowing up all their nuclear missiles ON THEIR OWN TERRITORY!!! Two weeks later, the radioactive clouds would work their way around to us and then...

Thank you for your thoughtful consideration,

DAVID CAPUTO

Appendix C

Print-outs from DEC's NOTES files on the World Bank and rainforest issue: This is a sample letter on Digital Corporation's *environmental issues* NOTES file:
Please feel free to use this sample letter.
December 7, 1988
Mr. Barber Conable
President, The World Bank
1818 H. St. S.W.
Washington D.C. 20433, USA

Dear Mr. Conable,

As a US citizen concerned about the destruction of tropical forests and the dislocation of indigenous peoples, I strongly object to the proposed POWER SECTOR II LOAN to Brazil, and specifically to the ALTIMARA HYDRO project, involving the KARAROA DAM on the Xingu River. My understanding is that this project would entail significant destruction of rainforest, not only due to flooding, but due as well to subsequent urbanization and settlement.

It is time that REAL priority be given to environmental factors in making investment decisions. At the rate the Brazilian rainforests are being destroyed, we can no longer afford to treat such destruction as an unfortunate side effect of economic expansion. The long-term environmental effects of projects which contribute to tropical deforestation must no longer be heavily discounted or treated as externalities.

I urge you to reject the proposed POWER SECTOR II LOAN to Brazil, to develop and adhere to investment criteria that make environmental preservation a priority, and to actively use your influence with governments such as Brazil to help stop destruction of the tropical rainforests.

Sincerely,

Letter from the GRATEFUL DEAD NOTES file "take my advice, you'd be better off Dead"
This is what I wrote to the Bank:

Dear Mr. Conable,

This is the first time I have ever written in protest of a certain action by any group, but when I read about the Power Sector II loan your bank is proposing to give Brazil, I had to write and say do not loan them the money. My reasons are as follows. First rain forests are a major source for the clean air we breathe and for possible medical cures. Also, rain forests around the world are being destroyed at alarming rates. This has to stop or we will endanger our own existence on this planet. If your bank loans Brazil this money, you are telling me and the American people you do not care about the planet's long-term future, only your company's short-term monetary concerns.

I urge you for myself, my wife, and my 3-month old son, please do not give Brazil the money: they want this loan to destroy the rain forest and uproot every living thing in that rain forest, including two tribes.

Sincerely, Robert Randall

Response to David Caputo's note on the rainforest issue from the

ALL PROCEEDS BENEFIT
BLACK SELF RELIANCE
PROGRAMS AT UHURU
HOUSE IN East OAKLAND
IN OAKLAND:
- black babies die at a rate 4½ times
  the rate of white babies
- there is 1 doctor for every 2,000
  black people AND 1 doctor for every
  200 white people
- over 10,000 people are homeless
- 90,000 malnourished mostly black
  women and children

It is in our interest as
white people to support
THE UHURU HOUSE PROGRAMS
FOR COMMUNITY CONTROL OF
HOUSING — HEALTH CARE
FOOD — AGAINST POLICE
BRUTALITY etc

Uhuru Foods is part of the
GROWING UHURU MOVEMENT.
WE ARE WHITE WORKERS WHO
WANT TO BUILD A NEW RELATIONSHIP
TO THE BLACK COMMUNITY, ONE
WHERE WE RAISE RESOURCES TO
GO TO THE BLACK COMMUNITY

Polish [Dead Head Special] Vegetarian
Sausage Specials
Foot Long Hot Dogs - Hot Coffee - Cold Soda
Giant Chocolate Chip Cookies
Apple Crumb Pie - Fudge Brownies
All Proceeds go to Uhuru House
Black Power Center in Oakland

GRATEFUL DEAD NOTES file:

RAINFOREST VICTORY! (The World Bank did not approve the Brazil loan)

David,

I commend you for your valor, and thank you for your efforts. I would not have known about this if it wasn't for you, and when I sent my letter, I was wondering if it would really make any difference. Well, seeing the results, I can't help but feel that I have done something good, and for once, ***it worked!!***

You have made my day, possibly my week/month.

Get up stand up
Stand up for your rights
Get up stand up
Don't give up the fight!
Don't give up the fight!

Press on my friend.

D.L.

Response to David Caputo's rainforest note in the ENVIRONMEN-TAL ISSUES NOTES, DEC:

Urgent! Save the rainforest

Right on! Now that's the kind of involvement I like to see in this notesfile! Nothing happens without pressure from concerned people. I have read about this project before. Its high time the Bank started giving REAL priority to the environment.

You mentioned some of the primary impacts of the project. The secondary impacts will be even worse, since the cheap power will attract settlement, and further urbanization, causing even more substantial deforestation.

Think I'll send off another letter to my dear friends at the bank right NOW.

a.f.

Appendix D

This article appeared in the first issue of "THE WEEKLY NEWS," an activist, underground newspaper based in Amherst, Massachusetts.

Rainforest Activist Murdered in Brazil

It is no longer a surprise to people that by disregarding and destroying our earth's tropical rainforest, we create major ecological disasters, reaching as far as heat waves and drought in western Massachusetts. Now that we have gripped onto this idea, we have to have the even more ugly realities of the forces behind the burning and felling of the rainforests. The number one cause of rainforest destruction is not cattle ranching, or logging, or overpopulation. Corrupt politics and capitalist systems are our direct link to the creation of the worst ecological and social disaster of this century and the next.

December 1988 finally brought an incident which began to slap Jane and Joe Average in the face with these facts. The leader of a great humanistic and environmental movement was murdered in Brazil. "Chico" Mendes, president of Amazonia's rubber tappers' movement, was assassinated by the shot of a rifle at point blank range on the back porch of his home, while two police guards waited for him in his kitchen. He was murdered by the wealthy cattle ranchers whom he opposed for their burning of the forest and for creating conditions of starvation for the local people who depended upon it to survive.

Mendes spent his life trying to disentangle his family, and the 30,000 other families who joined his efforts, from the poverty and slavery Brazil's rubber barons strapped on them over fifty years ago. He had been fighting for land and civil rights for the local peoples of Amazonia and for conservation of the rainforest which harbors the rubber trees from which they make their living. The Amazon's rubber tappers extract the latex from rubber trees as we do syrup from maples and sell and trade the produce for their food and income. The survival of the trees, and the rubber tappers, depends upon maintaining a sound, healthy rainforest. If tapped properly, "affectionately," in the words of Chico Mendes, the trees will provide latex for up to one hundred years. When a cattle ranch is cleared, nothing will grow after only five years. Conflicts over land rights and uses resulted in Mendes' death when the neighboring rancher ordered his assassination. The cattle ranchers' drive for profits claimed the lives of half a dozen other rubber tappers who intervened last year. Mendes was the first to draw attention. None of the killers have been charged.

Support for cattle ranching schemes in Amazonia have long been supported by the government. Favors are traded, land is given free, tax incentives assist the clearing of forest, and once the land has been "developed," speculators sell out to powerful multinationals. International loans from the World Bank or the Interamerican Development Bank usually pay for the initiation of such fiascoes. In short, our tax dollars pay for everything from burning the rainforest and boosting the "greenhouse effect," to paying Chico Mendes' assassin and those who have killed hundreds of other Brazilian peasants and Indians since the development of Amazonia began. In an interview two weeks before Mendes' death he said, "It is not that I would not die for the cause, but I intend to live a long time because a busy funeral will not make much difference." The best we can do to honor his life is to see to it that his death does make a difference.

Letters of protest about Chico Mendes' assassination and in support of the rubber tappers can be mailed to:
President Jose Sarney
Presidencia do Republica
Gabinete Civil, Palacio do Planalto
70150 Brasilia - DF, Brazil

Mr. Romeu Tuma
Superintendent Geral da Policia Federal
DPF: SAS Quadra 06 Proj 9/10
70070 Brasilia - DF, Brazil

Over breakfast on January 15, 1989, A new underground newspaper was formed. "The Weekly News" will be published every Thursday for the forseeable future. Our purpose is to bring the ignored truth to light, keep it in the light, and make sure something gets done about it. We are photocopier based. In the Soviet Union, dissidents often hand copy or type with carbon paper their publications. In the United States and some other affluent countries, we have the luxury of photocoping so we should take advantage of it. If you have access to a copying machine, subscribe to "The Weekly News". When you get it, photocopy it a couple of times and hand it out to your friends. If you work at an office, don't get yourself in trouble, but there is usually an acceptable level of personal use that is considered an unspoken fringe benefit. If you own a photocopier, then make lots of copies and leave them all over the place.

If you will make and distribute at least 2 copies you can have a free subscription. Just send us your address, and the approximate number that you will be able to make each week. If you can't make copies, then the mail-order subscription rate is whatever it costs to mail it plus any voluntary donation. We are seeking to file for tax-exempt status so anyone who has a matching grants system at work, like Digital does, can let us know and we will give you the nessecary information. We are also seeking submissions of any material for the publication. News stories, strange ads for facist pieces of equipment, comix strips, editorials, letters to the editor, photos, graphics, etc... This is an open-ended exercise in participatory journalisim. We do collective editing and try to become better writers as we practice. I hope you send us your address so that we may send you a free issue. Send all material to:

The Weekly News
Suite 227
56A Main Street
Maynard, MA 01754

The Greenpeace Movement

Laura Belanger

It has taken life on Earth 3.5 billion years to arrive at its present state. But now, with modern technology, what has taken billions of years to create can be destroyed in a few hours. Thousands of square miles of forest are destroyed every day. Entire species have become extinct. Toxic contaminants have found their way into our air, water, food supplies and even into our bodies. Many lakes, rivers and seas are so toxic they hold barely any life at all. While this gradual poisoning is obviously very frightening a more immediate threat exists. It is the ominous possibility of complete nuclear destruction. If we continue on our present course it is undeniable that irreversible damage will eventually destroy the beautiful world we know leaving the Earth a barren planet.

How can this be stopped when virtually every institution in our world is in some way tied into this system of ruination? These institutions, which include our governments, are unable to objectively observe the damage being inflicted. This has created an unwillingness to reverse the process and begin the necessary repair.

In the midst of all this madness there are people concerned about the Earth's fate. These people strongly believe the Earth and its creatures deserve better treatment than they have been receiving. They are committed to confronting offending institutions, whether big business or government, and demanding that changes be made.

In 1970 several of these people were protesting a United States Nuclear test which was to be held on the Canadian island of Amchitka. If allowed to take place this test would kill all of the land and marine life in the vicinity. The "Don't Make a Wave Committee"(1) was formed. Its intention was to sail a boat, the "Greenpeace" (named after the hope of creating an ecologically sound world), into the testing zone. This would force the test to be cancelled. Though numerous complications arose and it did not actually stop that particular test the committee had rallied the public to their cause. Pressure eventually caused President Nixon to call off all future tests at that site.

The women and men of the "Don't Make a Wave" committee had found that they could bring about change. Unfortunately after Amchitka, internal disagreements led to the disbandment of the committee. Still dedicated to their cause many of these same people decided to form a new group they called "Greenpeace". In their own words, "Greenpeace is an international organization dedicated to preserving the Earth and the life it supports. We work to stop the threat of nuclear war, to protect the environment from nuclear and toxic pollution, and to halt the needless slaughter of whales, dolphins, seals and other endangered animals."(2)

Greenpeace has effectively deterred many environmental offenders. After Amchitka activists in Greenpeace went on to end French nuclear testing in 1974 in the South Pacific skies above Murura(3). Subsequently they decided to incorporate the plight of whales into their campaigns. Through their efforts greater restrictions on whaling have been established. Greenpeace brought an end to the massacre of harp-seal pups by persuading Canada to outlaw the hunts in 1987. They have stopped the spraying of insecticides saving the lives of thousands of animals and keeping food and water supplies from becoming poisoned.(4) Greenpeace has challenged the practice of dumping nuclear waste into our seas. These are but a few examples representative of a multitude of Greenpeace victories.

Greenpeace offers a gleam of hope for our world. In its campaigns it seeks to arouse public outrage and use this as a weapon to right the wrongs it observes. Greenpeace relies solely on nonviolent direct action. By documenting offenders in action Greenpeace can inform communities of ongoing crimes. Concentrating public and political pressure often forces offenders to terminate their violations.

One of the reasons Greenpeace has been so triumphant is the devotion of its members. These are people willing to make tremendous sacrifices in their fight for an unmarred environment. The strategy in the "Save the Whales" campaign was to place Greenpeace members and their rubber inflatable rafts between the harpooners and the whales surfacing for air. Over a period of several years they have continuously confronted Japanese, Russian, Icelandic, and Australian whaling fleets in attempts to stop the slaughter of this peaceful and dwindling species.

In deterring sealhunters from bludgeoning the pups to death with their clubs activists shielded the seals with their bodies. Eventually they began spraying the seal's coats with bright colored dye. This makes the seal skin commercially valueless. To stop Britain from dropping barrels filled with nuclear waste into the Atlantic, rubber inflatable boats were critically positioned under the dumping areas. The British either had to stop dumping or risk serious injury to the person in the boat. In numerous campaigns this tactic has been utilized. It not only deters the offender but people recognize the sincerity of the rafters' commitment and come out in support of him/her. Attention is focused on the wrongs being committed and demands for changes are made.

As can be expected, Greenpeace has formed many enemies in its campaigns to make safety a primary consideration. Motivated by profit many governments and businesses would be much happier if Greenpeace were not in the picture. They sometimes try to assure this. In the conflict with France over the nuclear testing over Murura several Greenpeace members were beaten by French navymen. While in the rubber inflatable which was under the dumping shoot of a British boat the British dropped an enormous barrel of nuclear waste on a Greenpeace member(5). Luckily he was not seriously hurt. Perhaps the most upsetting instance was the sabotage of the Greenpeace boat the "Rainbow Warrior" which was sunk when the French secret service placed two mines on it. Photographer Fernando Pereira was killed in the explosion(6). The attack was a reaction to efforts being made to expose France's environmental abuses.

Only people strongly dedicated to a cause would risk such dangers. Aside from threat of bodily harm Greenpeacers continuously find themselves being arrested, fined and having their ships seized at port. These people go up against tremendous odds and often have to fight a battle that lasts many years. Often even when it seems as if they've won; a previous offender starts dumping, whaling, or testing as soon as public attention has shifted elsewhere.

Greenpeace is a nonprofit organization which depends entirely on public support. Through the sale of memberships and various promotional items, such as t-shirts, buttons, stuffed animals and films the revenue comes in. Greenpeace offers people a way in which we can participate in effective change.

Notes

1. Robert Hunter, *Warriors of the Rainbow* (Holt, Rinehart and Winston, New York, NY) 1979, p. 7
2. *Greenpeace introductory pamplet*, 1988
3. Hunter, p. 118
4. Ibid, p. 396
5. Greenpeace film, "*Greenpeace*"
6. "*Greenpeace*", volume 13, no.1, January-February 1988,p.4.

WOODCUT BY JEFF MORIN 162

the cookie jar

leigh brownhill

the head injury unit at bolton memorial was a busy place to be stuck on a thursday night. more than thirteen cases of severe head trauma were admitted and my scrapes were hardly noticed by the bustling attentive nurses and the slow-walking doctors who signed their names to the nurses' work. i couldn't seem to command any attention, but give up, i did not.

"i need a doctor," i cried, thinking the blood streaming down the side of my head and into my shirt collar would lend credence to my call. i felt like i was in vietnam. you know, those films they show of hundreds of wounded, and only three medics to take care of them all. i thought if i screamed in agony like those boys did, if i reached out a bloody hand and grabbed one of those clean, white coats; if only i could let them know how much i hurt. but no, the silent ones called much more attention to themselves. i, after all, could still speak, i could still stand, i was lucky. the silent, prone patients were definitely in need of more urgent care. even i could see that.

"here you go, dear", she said, and scurried away towards a mangled man who had just been rushed in. i stared at what resembled a human being and was struck at the powerlessness of the body beyond a certain mysterious stress point. i pondered this stress point of human capacity and drifted back to key largo, where stress is a hard thing to find in the natives; "conchs", they call themselves. i wondered if they could withstand a greater amount of stress upon their bodies because of their stress-free lives? or maybe less for the same reason. who knows.

i looked down to realize that the nurse had given me an ice pack wrapped in a bright white towel. i laughed at myself about the panic i had been in two hours before, blood streaming out of my scalp, matting my hair, covering the left side of my face with its red audacity. i'd heard about things like this, an aneurysm forms, victim dies twelve hours after being sent home from the emergency room with an ice pack. i was sure i was going to become the next case study at harvard med school. then they would all know about my mediocre diet, my habit of ingesting certain hallucinogens when i was in school. or what if they used my body as a model in an autopsy class? is there such a thing? those snobby, rich kids would see the hickey on the inside of my thigh from my monday night guest. they'd see the tattoo on my right shoulder blade of an ancient greek word for "love". (what i let my lovers talk me into!) i felt like such a wimp now and held the ice against my head. things like that didn't happen to nice people, like me.

it really did hurt, after all. but i suddenly felt so bourgeois, so middle-class. standing in my kitchen in an idiotic panic, with a broken cookie jar on the floor and blood starting to seep out of the cut, i called a taxi to pick me up and drive me to the hospital. manny was the driver's name. as i screamed my directions, he casually suggested, "rough night?" sure, now that i thought of it, it was a rough night, that's all. the ice pack was dripping now. i called myself another taxi and waited outside, hoping to see manny's brown face.

Social Causes of Virginia's Death.

Daria Casinelli

This editorial was originally printed in **Critical Times,** *a student-run left paper at UMASS, Amherst. The following letter and response appeared in a subsequent issue of* **Critical Times.** *Daria Casinelli is a graduate of the Social Thought and Political Economy Program at the University.*

This murder was not the sort that makes prime time viewers happy. Unlike t.v. cop dramas, there was no smoking gun, no secret motive, no underground drug deals and there is no way that anyone can explain what happened to Virginia Ferrer in half an hour to someone who's just killing time before the Cosby's come on. Understanding why Virginia Ferrer was killed by the boyfriend against whom she'd had six to twelve restraining orders means looking beyond our own fear, anger and ignorance to reasons that don't seem to have anything to do with murder.

The first thing we have to know is that there was more than one murderer in this case; there were three accomplices that everyone knew had the same intent as Allen Jose Reyes. Ferrer's eldest sister Correa told the Gazette, "He always said if she wasn't his, she wasn't anybody's". First the State, embodied in the Department of Social Services, the police and the courts, wanted Virginia to be a wife and mother, their kind of wife and mother. At this point it didn't even matter to them that she wasn't married, as long as she was connected to a man. DSS suggested that Virginia's children would be returned to her if she reunited with Reyes. In this way she would be their kind of woman, a woman with a man. The police are well known for refusing to arrest husbands or boyfriends who assault their wives, preferring to accept violence as part of a family remaining a family. And finally the courts, even in light of the case of Pam Nigro, a woman killed by her known abuser after a judge refused to give her another restraining order (the judge was investigated and removed from domestic abuse cases), still exhibit a bias against women, especially latinas, requesting restraining orders. Like Reyes, the intent of the State is to keep women, all women, bonded to a man.

What the State has to gain from keeping women married is, again, harder to see than what Allen Jose Reyes had to gain from keeping her, 'his'. But for starters it is much less expensive for the State to let hundreds of thousands of women strangle in violent poverty than to provide them with the income necessary to raise their children decently, something it need not do if they are 'partnered'. Dead is cheaper still.

The State is not the only monolith suspect in this crime. Statistics tell us that women make 69 cents for every dollar a man makes. Married women do far more of the unbenefitted part-time work in our country than men or single women. The economic system, capitalism, that creates an underpaid underclass is the second accomplice Virginia's murder. Its motive is profit.

You might say, but what about Reyes, what were his reasons, what are the human reasons for this murder? I don't know Reyes, his life or his reasons. I assume he is latino and low-income, but that doesn't tell me anything about his reasons, his personal reasons. What I do know about him is what many of the white women gathered at the candlelight vigil on the evening of September 13 know. We know that men commit more violent crimes than women, that men are raised in a culture that condones violence in general and laughs at violence against women. The system described above is populated predominantly by men and benefits men. Many of the women at the candlelight vigil for Virginia made it abundantly clear that they thought men were the problem, the murderers. But focussing on 'men' as the only problem makes us blind to the third accomplice to the murder of Virginia Ferrer; racism.

What many of the apparently middle and upper middle class and definitely white women at the vigil didn't know, or didn't acknowledge, was that the white system does violence to people of color everyday and that racism, in spite of the fact that all of the individual players in this drama were people of color, also killed Virginia. Racism permits the economically profitable tactic of divide and conquer. A divided workforce means the lowest wages and worst living conditions for women of color and slightly more for everyone each rung up the ladder of oppression. More poverty means more violence among those fighting to get one step up. No white person could ever say what racism meant in Virginia Ferrer's life, or to any person of color. What we can do, now, is identify all her murderers; Allen Jose Reyes, the State, the economic system and racism, and make sure none of them get away with it again.

The Letter:

Dear Sirs and Madames:

Congratulations for your paper *Critical Times* and more specifically your October issue! You have succeeded in giving UMass an important option to the hopeless wasteland of trendoid writing to be found in the Collegian.

However; please, in the future, try to avoid the Populist claptrap one sees in Miss Casinelli's cover essay "Who's to blame for Virginia Ferrer's Death". Miss Casinelli's absurdly unsupported generalizations are the sort of backyard tiresome polemics one sees all the time in a media which thrives on men bashing and mis-information.

It was very late Friday night but I decided to take my normal route from the UMass police parking lot thru Thompson and Machmer and out to the Student Union Building. This particular

night a woman followed me into the building. I was feeling a little misanthropic so as soon as I realized she was behind me I quickened my pace, that's how I knew right away that she had also started walking faster. By the time I got to the first turn in Thompson I could see her over my shoulder, no one I knew. She saw me and stopped. I thought that was a little weird but not that weird. I kept going and she kept going, I went faster and she went faster, thru the connecting corridor and into Machmer and still she didn't overtake me until my boot came untied by the Coke machine. I stooped down to tie it and she flew past, determined to get past me and on with her business.

Someone might remind Miss Casinelli that Domestic Violence (sic) is a two way street and that while Mrs. Ferrer's death was sad and unfortunate, the homicide rate between the married sexes has remained equal for the past fifty years! Wives kill husbands equally as often as husbands kill wives. Are the police well known for refusing to arrest boyfriends and husbands who assault their wives? Prove it. I would suggest the opposite- that due process goes by the boards. In the December 21 issue of *Time*, it was glowingly reported that a new

Charlestown, S.C. police dept. policy, under which men accused of domestic violence are arrested at their places of work, "to make the collar sting". The idea that this may destroy an innocent mans reputation and livelihood has not crossed the minds of either these police or *Time* magazine, though things not crossing the minds of *Time* magazine reporters is hardly surprising.

Early in the morning, six a.m. I saw the man who all summer rips down feminist posters all over Amherst. Something about them makes him so angry he rips them down in gusts of fury, he laughs like a maniac and doesn't notice that I'm watching. Are you that man?

Another point in Miss Casinelli's article was the judge not returning Mrs. Ferrer's children until she was reunited with Mr. Reyes. Admittedly, I'm not familiar with the particulars, however, I assume that the judge removed the children from Ferrer because they were in danger and he hoped that the presence of a male figure would offer some protection for them. The judge was monstrously wrong in this case but 70 percent of all child abuse *is* inflicted by women and the presence of men in households may inhibit the violent behaviors of women towards children.

On campus posters for feminist events are written on by the same man with the same red marker for months on end, including one's outside my door. The poster for an EWC support group on lesbian battering says, "Sympathy for the she-devils", the flyer for the Socialist ~Feminism discussion group says, "Stop Male Bashing". Are you that man?

I agree with Miss Casinelli that our culture condones violence in general, however, I would say that it laughs a little harder at violence against men ... for instance, the 6 o'clock news reports that a man is raped by a woman (sic) at gunpoint. This is comedy to many. It's just too funny that a man could be made to do such a thing. An uncommon example, but useful to illustrate the seemly scarcity of domestic violence against men. Men are clearly not eager to report that they've been abused by their wives, because they'll be ridiculed. *Time* tells us not to worry though, "because they are smaller, women are less likely to inflict more damage". They may wish to consider the equal murder rates between husbands and wives or possibly the 1984 M. Mc-

Leod study (Women against Men: An Examination of Domestic Violence, *Justice Quarterly*, I pp. 171-193) "Although 25% of all other offenses against women were classified as aggravated assaults, and the vast majority of the latter cases involved the use of weapons." McLeod concluded that "Clearly violence against men is much more destructive than violence against women ... Male victims are injured or often and more seriously than are female."

Late Saturday night I'm walking thru Thompson to get to Machmer to get to the Student Union building to type my very late piece for Critical Times. A man follows me into the building, so I walk faster and he walks faster. At the first corner I swing wide so that I can see him, but he looks down, still I don't think its anyone I know. I walk faster but now I can't see him because I've passed thru the first door. He must've paused for a second because I'm in the middle of the connecting corridor and he still hasn't come thru the doors. 'Good', I think, 'I'll sprint the rest, just for the hell of it and he'll never know.' I start off, my steps ringing so loud in the empty building that I'm almost to the Coke machine before I realized there are two sets of echos; he's

running too. I run faster, thru the fifth set of doors where my oh-so-brave-boots trip me up. I fall, paralyzed with terror, 'There's a man chasing me.' The three women I know who've been raped appear before me, "Get up!, Get up!", they say. I lurch forward and hurtle thru the rest of the building not pausing until I reach the Student Union steps. He stops in the doorway and goes in another direction. Were you that man?

Perhaps, *Time* is aware of these realities but is also aware of the fact that they are not only good copy but are genuine bits of real controversy they deem to (sic) caustic for the reading public to swallow. This is sad, in that, if any semblance of gender sanity is to be achieved the public must not be spoon fed the popular but rather must be led to reality, where they may digest it any way they choose.

letter by John F. Gibney

response (in bold type) by Daria Casinelli

MEET JANE
an anti racist-
anarcha- socialist-
feminist collective

The Jane Doe Liberation Front:

A Statement of Principles

The following statement is a brief introduction to some of Jane's values and goals. Jane strives for a comprehensive analysis of the oppression of all women and a strategy that addresses this oppression in all its forms. We believe in a historically based perspective of the human condition, that it is in constant flux and that our understanding of our physical, social, and psychological selves are functions of our specific age, race, gender, culture, economy and time period.

We feel, especially, that racism, patriarchy and capitalism function both together and autonomously to oppress all women and men, that none is more or less important than the other and all work together in a complicated web of destructive power relations. We think it is valid to separate all three in order to recognize their individual patterns and to understand them better: we also think it is crucial to remember that these systems create a web of oppression whose very power lies in their interconnection.

White racism is a cultural institution which mandates the inferiority of people of color economically, sexually, politically, and socially. For example, our educational system and the media are two powerful social tools which

170

define what is important and what is known. These institutions of the state and the economically powerful are controlled primarily by white people and create a distorted and lopsided view of who, as a society or culture, we are, what we need, and what we value.

In this male dominated society, male defined individual and social priorities confine women to the role of primary caregiver, mistress, babymaker, wife, mother, fantasy object and commodity. Economically this translates into women functioning as unpaid or low paid labor or in unskilled and semiskilled jobs. Patriarchy maintains and celebrates compulsory heterosexuality in order to uphold the dominance of men: this confines the acceptable life choices of women to marriage, motherhood, male/female families and requires the violent suppression of lesbian existence and bisexuality.

We also advocate decentralizing power through community/public ownership and development of the major means of production; for instance, the banking system, the phone company, utilities and other production that fulfills basic human needs, i.e. food, housing, childcare. This means we would like economic priorities to reflect human needs rather than create false needs in the market based on the accumulation of goods simply for the profit making of a few. We do, however, respect a plurality of ideas and ways of producing a variety of goods and services which are needed in a healthy society which serves everyone. So, we have no plans for ravaging your Uncle George's barber shop but are interested in decentralizing the power now held by large corporations who work in conjunction with the state in focusing our economy on the accumulation of wealth for the few who already have it.

We feel it is important that a socialized economy operate on a local level so that people have direct opportunity to influence and create the work they do, to decide how they want to do it, and how best to serve all the people in their community. Because of the racism, sexism, classism, homophobia, and ablism that now exist in our society, we understand that changing the economic system alone would not guarantee the safety of women or people of color or address the specific needs and desires of this variety of people who are basically invisible in a culture dominated by white and male values. Therefore, we recognize the need to have some sort of checks and balances system that would protect the rights of all people throughout the whole country to have a decent standard of living and a dignified quality of life. We view this as a tension between national governments from which just and uniform standards could arise, and local power, where people have a direct voice in their own state of affairs. The present system of federal, state and local control addresses this somewhat, but we feel it is inadequate and does not maximize democratic possibilities. Yet, we feel torn about how we would envision a more just and truly democratic society that is not belabored by the bureaucracy and power struggles we see happening now.

As we mentioned at the beginning this is just a brief overview of what Jane is all about. There's a small membership rigmarole; a little study and a little talk. If you're interested, speak to Jane.

Daria Casinelli is a founding member of the Jane Doe Liberation Front. This statement of principles was written collectively by the group.

Children of the Homeless

Jane Devine

"My babies are just as smart and beautiful and good as other babies. They've survived times that would try the soul of the strongest man and they're just little kids."

"My job as a human being is to say 'I love you' until my last breath."

"There are hundreds of thousands of precious and irreplaceable resources in homeless shelters across this land."

These quotes are excerpts from Ella McCall's play *Voices From the Street*. Jane Devine is a graduate of the Social Thought and Political Economy Program and was a member of the Junior Seminar. She works at a local homeless shelter, where she shot the photographs on the following pages.

Celia loves to go to school, maybe she will go to college and do something nice with her life.

"I want to go to school to become a ballerina and dance on the stage to make alot of money to help my mother and grandmother."

"I wish to search for my mother and sisters and hug them and be happy. I also want to search for whales."

"I want to be a boy. I want to play."

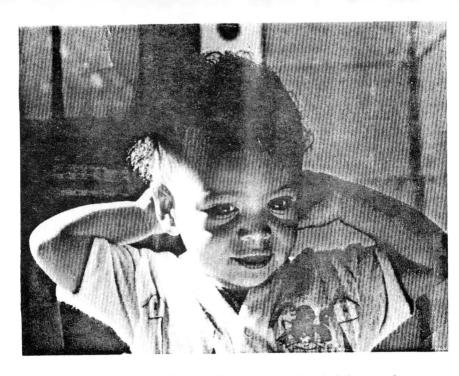

"I hope my daughter will go to college and study what she is interested in. She likes music, dancing and gymnastics."

Gathering Force

Taciana Ribero

I just believe in myself now.

I went through a lot of pain, it was very painful, but I also came out victorious, so I'm very strong and I really believe in myself. I was battered in my marriage to Mark. I didn't have any self-esteem, I didn't believe in myself. I didn't believe that I could do it on my own. The reason I didn't leave him before was, mostly, a struggle finacially. I didn't know how to live without being supported by Mark. How could I do it? I didn't know how to do it. There is nothing in the world that's ever going to stop me. I just believe in myself now. I know what I'm capable of and I know that nothing is ever going to stop me again. I don't think I'm every going to have such a hard time in life again. I think I had my fill.

I am a single mother from South America and a student at the University of Massachusetts, majoring in Social Thought and Political Economy. Sometimes I work in a textile factory and model for art classes. I was battered and now do workshops on violence against women. In 1989 we are helping some men start their own group to deal with men who beat and psychologically abuse women. In the workshops we read poems including the ones here:

Formerly Your Neighbor

Do you remember me?
I lived around the corner,
Across the street and
next door to you.
We weren's close, of course,
But we were neighborly.
We went to work,
Drove kids to school and
games and dance,
Our own and each other's,
And chatted when we met
About our homes, our lawns --
diapers, drapes, stemware
supermarket specials --
And other superficial things.
We never failed to wave and smile
As we passed.
Do you remember that
We exchanged seasons greetings
And several party invitations?
We were good neighbors
In good neighborhoods.
Now do you remember me?
I am the battered woman
Who lived with her children
In pain and terror
Around the corner,
Across the cul de sac
And next door to you.
  -**Barbara J. Cox**
   Fayetteville, Arkansas

Torture

When they torture your mother
plant a tree
When they torture your father
plant a tree
When they torture your brother
and your sister
plant a tree
When they assassinate
your leaders
and lovers
plant a tree
When they torture you
too bad
to talk
plant a tree.

When they begin to torture
the trees
and cut down the forest
they have made
start another.

Comes the Dawn

After a while you learn the subtle difference
Between holding a hand and chaining a soul
And you learn that love doesn't mean leaning
And company doesn't mean security
And you begin to understand that kisses aren't contracts
And presents aren't promises
And you begin to accept defeats with your head held high
And your eyes open
With the grace of a woman, not the grief of a child
You learn to build your roads
On today because tomorrow's ground
is too uncertain for plans and futures have
A way of falling down in mid-flight
After a while you learn that even sunshine
Burns if you get too much
So you plant your own garden and decorate
Your own soul, instead of waiting
For someone to bring you flowers
And you learn that you really can endure
That you really are strong
And you really do have worth
And you learn and learn and you learn
With every goodbye you learn

    -Veronica A. Shoffskall

I Am a Dangerous Woman

I am a dangerous woman
Carrying neither bombs nor babies
Flowers nor molotov cocktails.
I confound all your reason, theory, realism
Because I will neither lie in your ditches
Nor dig your ditches for you
Nor join in your armed struggle
For bigger and better ditches.
I will not walk with you nor walk for you.
I won't live with you
And I won't die for you.
But neither will I try to deny you
Your right to live and die.
I will not share one square foot of this earth with you

While your're hell-bent on destruction.
But neither will I deny that we are of the same earth,
Born of the same Mother.
I will not permit
You to bind my life to yours
But I will tell you that our lives
Are bound together
And I will demand
That you live as though you understand
This one salient fact.

I am a dangerous woman
Because I will tell you, sir,
Whether you are concerned or not.
Masculinity has made of this world a living hell,
A furnace burning away at hope, love, faith, and justice.
A furnace of My Lais, Hiroshimas, Dachaus.
A furnace which burns the babies
You tell us we must make.
Masculinity made "femininity,"
Made the eyes of our women go dark and cold,

Send our sons - yes sir, our sons -
To war,
Made our children go hungry,
Made our mothers whores,
Made our bombs, our bullets, our "Food for Peace,"
Our definitive solutions and first-strike policies.
Masculinity broke women and men on its knee,
Took away our futures,
Made our hopes, fears, thoughts and good instincts
"Irrelevant to the larger struggle,"
And made human survival beyond the year 2000
An open question.

I am a dangerous woman
Because I will say all this,
Lying neither to you nor with you
Neither trusting nor despising you.
I am dangerous because
I won't give up or shut up.
Or put up with your version of reality.
You have conspired to sell my life quite cheaply,
And I am especially dangerous
Because I will never forgive nor forget
Or ever conspire
To sell your life in return.

-Joan Cavanagh

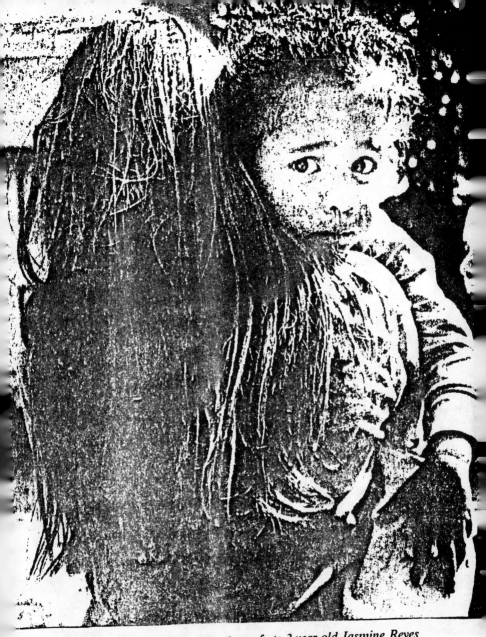

Tonia Gary, 11, of Avenue A comforts 3-year-old Jasmine Reyes (facing front), whose mother was murdered Friday night in Turners Falls.

Photo: Greenfield Recorder/Paul Franz

These women were among 300 people who gathered for a candlelight vigil to commemorate the death of Virginia Ferrer.

Photo: Richard Carpenter/Hampshire Daily Gazette

criticism, modeling, and v-ching, or (in the case of my wayward roommate) and to more power relations between people of different ar-
guments races and classes during school recess periods. Above all, in
these new schools, if 1960s politics teach us anything, we learned
what it meant to feel the pain. It was a risk to our resolve into
the world of power, we were on to until ... 1 hit limit toward

187

Collective Desk Top Publishing:

How We Did What We Did

Jose Afonso, Matthew Collins, Leigh Brownhill, Terisa Turner, Erin Crawley, Timothy Belknap, Amy Pearson

"First you need some people who will each write a chapter. Then you need some word processing equipment and a desktop publishing program. This is easy. The challenge is to see the process through from beginning to end with perseverance, good faith, and a ruthless editorial eye."

Collectivity

Who are we? All are majors in a special degree at the University of Massachusetts called Social Thought and Political Economy. This program is interdisciplinary, and many of the required courses are honors courses. All majors must take a two semester core curriculum called the Junior Seminar in Social Thought and Political Economy. Our junior seminar first met in February 1988. Terisa Turner team taught the February - May 1988 semester with Ted Norton. In our second semester, September - December 1988, Terisa taught us herself. There were seventeen of us and we began the year together with a bang. Two weeks after class started in February 1988 the building where we met, New Africa House, was occupied by black students and their supporters. We were in the middle of this fight back against racism and sexism. In the first semester we read classical texts and commentaries from four historical epoches: hunting and gathering; precapitalist societies; early capitalism and late capitalism. We tried to be global, and to trace power relations between people of different genders, races and classes during each of these periods of history. In the second semester we tried to put this theoretical and historical knowledge into practice. Our practice was to make an intervention into the world of print. We wrote two books. The first, *Voices of the*

Twentieth Century: Our Foremothers Speak, was interviews with our grandmothers around two questions: relations with your boss and relations with your spouse. The second book is this one: *Revolutionary Popular Culture*.

My Part in Publishing and Writing

"Creating the book Revolutionary Popular Culture was a collective effort, therefore each class member could chose any number of roles having to do with the completion of the book. I chose a relatively active role. Besides researching and writing on the subject of Jamaican farm workers in the U.S., I also played the part of an editor. My duties included, among other things, accompanying a small group of class members along with Professor Turner to New York City for a working weekend field trip. There in New York with the aid of Jim Murray, the curator of the C.L.R. James Institute, we became well versed in the art and language of desk top publishing. Using the Ventura Desk Top Publishing soft-ware on an IBM personal computer, we were able to produce a high quality, graphically pleasing manuscript. Learning this process was significantly empowering because we were able to transform what we had typed onto a computer screen into a marketable piece of literature. To be sure there were many other activities that went into the process of book making. Much of the work involved investigation. We went out in search of technology. For instance, at the University of Massachusetts Press we found a way to convert photographs into a photo-copyable image using a special machine. Jim Murray introduced us to Ventura desktop publishing, the University Computing Center introduced us to word processing, and a private firm along with UMASS Duplicating introduced us to the method of perfect binding."

"If It Don't Feel Good..."

I wanted to get away from cynicism. I wanted to enjoy resources and to confront power in all our relations. The work process with all its ups and downs, was our terrain for fighting out issues of power especially between people with technical skills and those without. This was a fight between men and women to a great extent. New ways of interacting to overcome sexism and our socialized conceptions of what is women's work and what is men's work were pursued. Class issues were tied into the work process. If you are rich, and your Daddy sends you money, you don't have to work in a shit job, earning minimum pay, getting exhausted, serving the public or taking trips from your supervisor or boss. You have more time for the process of writing the book, and you may be distanced from the majority who do have to follow a strict work schedule. Participants from upper middle class, professional families struggled with inequality. Many gave of their resources and time very freely and consciously, sometimes within a liberal mindset, sometimes in the context of deliberate class suicide. A challenge was to lock the project's logistics and morality into the day-to-day realities of the working class students in the group. Only students know the intimacies of this reality, and only students could keep the work on course, on the people's track. A socialized work process is what we tried to operate in writing *Voices* and *Revolutionary Popular Culture*. *How can that* function and flourish in a an opportunistic, careerist milieu where students are pitted against each other, fighting for highest grades and for seats in over-crowded, limited-attendance classes? Probably the two key methods we used with success were, first:

> the development of universally recognized skills
> and their application to producing a product that
> is available for public evaluation;
> and second:
> the unrelenting priority given to enjoyment.

We fought for socialist practice, in the capitalist 'star wars boom economy' heartland; by undergoing training in intellectual production and by having genuine, high grade fun doing it.

What We Did

Our class made all of its decisions through consensus. This was a major factor in the construction of community around the synthesis of our book. We believe that this community was essential to the quality and quantity of work we put into the book.

Class was never constrained to the limitations of the classroom. We met more often outside of class than in. Dr. Terisa Turner, our professor, and our classmates met at each others' houses to do our work. We congregated at dorms, using rooms to drop off and pick up materials. Many of us spent time at Terisa's house on Lake Pleasant. One of us might spend eight hours in editorial session, working with Terisa or another student, getting our text in shape. There was no separation of work and play. Since working on the book meant so much to us, it was a part of our lives, and we had loads of fun doing it. We lived for what we were doing, we were not doing something for a living.

The Technology is Ours to Use

We are strong believers in the power of technology. It can have power over us, but we can also appropriate it to fight power relations. We are about harnessing technology for social change and revolution. We used computers to the fullest extent that we could. What took years to develop, can be learned in a few hours time. Regular people of all sorts can learn how to write using the computer. Granted, these people will need access to computers, though this access is spreading. We who have the hardware and skills can put them at the disposal of people who don't, here and abroad. One can type up a document and have it printed the next day in several different countries around the world. This is international power.

We used the University Computing Center [UCC] labs to do most of our actual writing. UCC provided us with lab time and first rate instruction. Microsoft Word Version 4.0 was our word processing software. Since each one of us was working on our own individual chapter, we each spent quite a bit of time in the labs. Some of us have our own word processors. More participants had access to friends' equipment.

We typed our chapters into the word processor, using ordinary organization of the material on the page. For instance, we would double space between paragraphs. Then we would get some editorial attention from Terisa and from one of the other seminar participants. The variation in this editorial experience was rich. Some chapters look almost exactly like their first or early drafts. Some chapters are totally re-thought and re-written. Sometimes new ideas were included to contextualize graphics, or to bounce off of themes in different chapters. For most of us, the writing part was the most intense and fun.

We worked on other people's chapters as well as our own. We tried to write for certain people. For instance, we tried to write for our younger brothers and sisters. Rachel and Joe actually wrote a letter to Rachel's eleven year old brother (chapter one, "*Making things to kill people at the university*"). Or we tried to write in a way that our grandmothers' would appreciate. We were thinking of our classmates reading the book, and we wrote for other students. Many of our chapters have been presented to lecturers and students in other classes or seminars. We got feedback from this broader readership.

Two chapters involved transcribing casette tape recordings of talks. This work was facilitated by using dictaphones that slow down the tape's speed to allow the editors of those chapters to type at a realistic rate. The transcribed talks were then re-worked to make them clear in a reading mode. This was a tremendous amount of work but it has produced the Donna Coombs chapter ("Women and recession in petroleum exporting societies: the case of Trinidad and Tobago") and the CLR James chapter ("On America"). We think these are two of the most valuable contributions which *Revolutionary Popular Culture* is making. Both chapters are by third world revolutionary intellectuals. They are published here for the first time.

After fixing up the text according to both content and style editing, we put in the kind of layout in the text that the desktop publishing program likes. For instance, we took out an extra paragraph return (a line) between paragraphs. We put one, not two spaces between sentences. We put 'tags' on subtitles so the publishing program would know to make the subtitle big and bold. Each one of us had a diskette with our chapter on it. So in the end, we put all the chapters on one diskette and headed down to our friend, Jim Murray's place in New York to use his Ventura Publishing software.

Ventura Publishing is one amazing program, and we are indebted to Jim Murray for processing our work through it. Ventura basically took our text from Microsoft Word and made it look like a **real** book. Ventura printed out our text sideways on half a sheet of paper. This was the orientation that we wanted for our book. Ventura added amazing design features where they were wanted and uniformity where it was needed. The products that came out of Ventura Publishing were printouts of each of our chapters, each different, yet the titles and authors were printed the same throughout the book. We also printed out all other parts of the book and page numbers so that we could, by hand, put the book together to be reproduced.

Photographs

Our skills and the technology we used for the photographs improved drastically. For the first book, we used straight photocopies of pictures of our foremothers. We cut them down to the right size for the book, too. We got great results considering the technology we used. John even took a mini-course in developing black and white film and printing a photograph he took of his mother. The pictures in the first book, *Our Foremothers Speak*, were in tune with the subject and form. They were family snap shots, some of them very old. And the photocopy reproduction emphasized this funky homeness. We did not want to be slick.

For the second book, we were able to use the "half-toning" process for our pictures. The more sharply black and white the pictures are, the better they come out. If you are printing your own pictures, you probably will want to use a light filter to get more black-white contrast. What the half-toning process does is break our photographs down into dots, especially the grey areas. What does this do? When the half-tone image is reproduced using photocopying it comes out at a much higher level of quality than could be produced by photocopying the picture straight. The half-toning process is what newspapers use. If you look very closely at newspaper photos, you can see the dots.

Our thanks to the various publishing offices for their excellent instructions about how to do half-toning. We put the labor in, and in some cases, reimbursed them for the materials we used. Under the umbrella of "photos" we include graphics, photocopies of comics, drawings and everything else that is not words. These we got from our favorite publications, from artist friends, from ourselves and from post cards. Very helpful are the top quality self-serve photocopy machines in the copy shops in Amherst (or anywhere). We could make the illustrations bigger or smaller, lighter or darker. Some of us never made a poster or any illustrated page before. Others had much experience. We taught each other and we all now know how to make advertisements, book covers and graphics pages with the technology readily available in a good photocopy shop (light table, reduction and enlargement photocopy machine, paper cutter, tape or glue stick, scissors, typewriter, GBC binder, and other standard equipment). Not only can we all do these tasks that are vital to communication. We also have an attitude toward them. Usually these tasks are downgraded in value. They are left for secretaries or office assistants or (in a more traditional world) 'the girls' to do. We have a different appreciation: everybody gains from knowing how to do cutting and pasting and document production. And someone who cannot quickly generate a poster or publishable illustration lacks an important skill. When we finished the photos, and had all the Ventura printouts, we were ready to do the actual putting together of the book, so that it could be reproduced.

The "Mock-up" and the "Paste-up"

The "Mock-up" process is the first try at putting together the book. This requires much patience. The idea is to get everything together taking into account where the photographs and chapters will go. The book has to be sent to the printer basically as a flattened out book, that if folded down the middle, and both sides lifted together, can be read as the actual book. As you look down on the flattened out book, the two pages exactly in the middle of the book look up at you. The mock-up process requires much patience because as soon as you think you've got everything together perfectly; you've either forgotten a photo or come up with an extra page somewhere at the end.

Well, when the "Mock-up" was finished, we double checked everything and pasted all the pictures and everything else together. The end result is this packet where the two middle pages of the book are facing up, and the front and back covers are facing down, with all the other pages pasted in order in between. The pages with text on them are stuck onto the front and backs of all of the mounting pages. This is the "Paste-up".

Funding, Class Contacts and Footwork

Everyone in the class had contacts that were necessary for the production of the book. The biggest consideration was the funding of our book. Our first book had to be funded by pre-printing sales, and a few members of the class who were willing to front the money. Our second book was funded mostly by a short-term loan from our Social Thought and Political Economy program, from the sales of our previous book, and from advance sales of *Revolutionary Popular Culture*.

Advanced sales went well because we made a book cover with quotations from some of the chapters printed on it, just like on the back of this book. So people could see from these 'pull-quotes' something of the tenor of the text and many liked it and put down five dollars, instead of the projected bookstore price which is about seven dollars. A significant pre-paying group were students in other seminars in Social Thought and Political Economy, and students in Women's Studies who were being taught by Terisa and who were using the book in their courses. *Revolutionary Popular Culture* has a large number of authors. Most of us have friends and family who want a copy of our book. This added numbers to the advance sales. We learned that it was very easy to forward sell the book by giving each of the seminar participants about twelve specially made receipts. Each of us would sell a book, give the buyer half the receipt and keep the other half containing the buyer's name and address and phone number, and an indication of whether the buyer would get the book through the mail (add fifty cents to purchase price) or through the office of the Social Thought and Political Economy Program. It is necessary to emend space before: seminar people in the office to both forward sell to buyers who come there, and to handle the distribution of books to early buyers. This relieves additional workloads on office staff.

Essential contacts were the ones which allowed us access to printing information, computers, and inexpensive or free resources. There were many tasks that we needed to do. These were split up amongst the class, depending on time constraints of each individual. Some of us have to work in waged jobs less, and thus have more time free. Others have time-consuming courses or family obligations. We worked it out. Realistically.

ISBN Number, Library of Congress and Copyrights

We contacted our local publishers on how to deal with getting an international standard book number (ISBN) and a Library of Congress number. Kassahun Checole, publisher at Africa World Press in Trenton N.J., explained the ISBN system to us. The ISBN and Library of Congress numbers were sent to us after we applied on forms which are available from a company called Bowker in New York or through many publishing firms. The ISBN numbers are free. We got a whole list of ISBN numbers to use for all of our future books. The importance of ISBN and Library Congress numbers cannot be overstated. Anyone around the world can get a copy of our book with the ISBN number and it appears in the directory, *Books In Print*.

Some people have asked us why the publisher is the International Oil Working Group Inc. (IOWG) from New York. Because we wanted ISBN numbers, we needed to have an incorporated entity to which the numbers would be accorded. Terisa happens to be a director of the International Oil Working Group, a not for profit corporation which helps to enforce the oil embargo against South Africa. The IOWG is registered with the United Nations Department of Public Information in New York and is thereby part of the United Nations non governmental organization community. Since the IOWG had published documents before and given its political and educational, we thought it appropriate to publish the book under its name. *The international distribution of Revolutionary Popular Culture* will be easier because of the reputation of the IOWG in anti-apartheid and oilworker networks. This was practical too because Terisa as director of the IOWG, could approve what it was that we wanted to publish. There was no need for us to incorporate ourselves, or to negotiate the acceptability of our text with the directors of any other publishing group.

When we copyrighted the book, we made provisions that it could be reproduced for educational purposes. The book is intellectual property and it belongs to us, which is why we copyrighted it. But we are about sharing it freely with people who want to use it to learn or to do politics. We want this kind of free reproduction because we see an inherent need for as many people as possible to read our book, regardless of international borders or language. We did restrict reproduction for other uses because we see no reason why some rip-off artist or tycoon of capitalism should make money on our book.

A Note About Evaluation and Grades

This book and our previous book, <u>Voices of the Twentieth Century</u>, were collective efforts on the part of the Social Thought and Political Economy Junior Seminar taught by Terisa Turner. The structure of the class was egalitarian. Terisa was our professor, but she was involved in the project no more or less than we were as her students. To promote the collectivity that was necessary for such an undertaking, there could be no unequal reward system that might infringe on our ability to work as equals. Therefore, we rejected the university grading system.

As a group we decided that each of us would give as much as our schedules and capacities could allow. We agreed from the beginning that we would all receive A/B's. We made provisions that those who put in extra time and effort would receive A's. The extra recognition was supposed to go to people who helped others learn and grow, and who acted collectively. Three people were nominated for this distinction. This we decided through concensus at the end of the semester. The students who received the A grades clearly put in extra time and effort. Likewise, the students who chose not to fully participate in the class would be allotted lower grades. Students who could not complete projects were offered alternative projects to do. If these students, in turn, failed to complete these projects, then their grades dropped a full grade for each incomplete project. This matter we left up to our professor's discretion.

But it so happened that everyone made this class an essential part of their lives, working to extraordinary capacity. Thus no lower grades were needed. We found that a work process characterized by consensus was efficient. It produced work remarkable both for its quality and its quantity. We were recognized both privately, through the grades we received, and publicly through the response from critics, our families, and our peers.

Grading practice has everything to do with (a) relations of power between teacher and taught; (b) relations among students in the seminar and (c) relations between the student and the curriculum. We provide this information about grading in the hope that debate about the link between evaluation methods and quality education can incorporate our experience. We know that straight out grading by the teacher on the assumption that each student is equally able to learn or achieve, is dubious. The assumption of equal capacity ignores the advantages that whites, males, upper class people and wealthier students have over people of color, women, working class people and students struggling with finances. Straight professorial grading can penalize students who are women, black, poor and over-worked. We found that our evaluation system (and the 'each one teach one' practice) began to solve this institutionalized discrimination.

The Politics of Desktop Publishing

On December 15, 1988 seminar participants and our friends were upstairs at *Food For Thought Books* in downtown Amherst. We were having a party to celebrate the publication of our first book, *Voices of the Twentieth Century: Our Foremothers Speak.* The previous Friday most of us were at a reggae dance in Northampton's Center for the Arts where *The Loose Caboose* and *Rude Girls* were doing a benefit for Nicaragua after the hurricane. We spent a great deal of time in the art gallery outside the reggae party writing statements about what we thought of the first book and the process of getting it together. What we wrote we gave to Jose Afonso, of the seminar. He worked on it. What he came up with surprised many of us. At our own book party Jose got people's attention and read the following statement: The Social Thought and Political Economy Junior Seminar II class would like to thank all those individuals who offered us their assistance, time, and encouragement throughout the many chaotic periods of this project. We are indebted to Jim Murray whose knowledge of computer technology facilitated our efforts, to Professor John Bracey whose sympathetic words moved us to concentrate our struggles, and most of all to Terisa Turner, an extraordinary teacher, mentor, friend, and sometimes the most brutal editor who provided us with lots of inspiration, direction, focus, and understanding.

This project effectively exposed us to the real capabilities of the computer. The concept of desk-top publishing has been made available to students. It is now up to us to maximize to potential of this idea. We have been able to undermine the elitism of publishing. We hope to send shivers through the Professorial ranks of this institution and thus to effectively challenge other classes to demand that their professors teach them how to publish information. All students should be exposed to the idea of information exchange.

History, literature, and political poetries have long been monopolized by the elitist Phd's or the tenured tyrants. We have been subjected to a concept of history that, for the most part, originates from a top-bottom scheme. Desk-top publishing will empower us to expose the hierarchy of publishing. It will allow us to transcribe history from the grass roots level. We will be able to bring this technology to the neighborhoods, to the households, to the people. History will be revolutionized once we can make it a reflection of the people; it must express a bottom-top scheme for it to truly represent a people's history.

This project has unclothed a hidden avenue for students, for social activists, and for concerned members of the society. "Our Foremothers Speak" was a wonderful and enlightening experience. This book allowed us the opportunity to visit our past, to visit the very foundation of our identity, of our persona. Our foremothers have to be understood before we can even attempt to understand ourselves. We hope that their voices were able to transcend the pages, for they have long been neglected by the inflated egos of traditional historians. Thank you.

The Task Force On Desktop Publishing

Our writing group and the Southeast Street writing group has joined together to make the Task Force for desktop publishing. We have asked the people who supported our first book to lend their names to the task force. The Task Force is inspired by the principles outlined in Jose's statement above. And we continue to appropriate technology for communication on the people's track. The task force is an intersecting of networks. By design, it is not very formal. This desktop publishing work we believe to be consistent with the best of university education. It is clear that students embrace it, or variations on the theme, with enthusiasm and tenacity. We know some professors will learn from us and contribute their own knowledge and dedication. We know that desktop publishing in a collective spirit is part of a solid education. Other students are already using these books as models with positive and negative lessons to teach. Each of us has gained confidence and recognition. We can go on to organize and complete other total projects; whether in jobs, graduate school or our communities.

The Task Force came into existence in practice in September 1988 when our seminar started to do our book on grandmothers' lives. But it was only as we were coming to the end of doing the second book that the formal name, 'task force' was voiced in a New York dinner party. Seven of us were on a fieldtrip to New York in January 1989 to learn about publishing and to do some of the work on this book. We were finishing the one year junior seminar, and going our separate ways. The task force would represent some continuity. It would also enable us to continue publishing materials from other classes, from other activities and groups, and especially from other countries. Revolutionary popular culture, as defined in this book, has to do with international action that is both subversive and creative. The taskforce could be part of this process.

The following thoughts about this task force represent initial discussions over the first few weeks of 1989. Without question, the ideas will change and ways of doing task force work will emerge from the collectivity. What would be good and what would not be good for collective desktop publishing will also be clarified. It is clear that a direction has been set and there is no turning back: desk top publishing by students and their allies is going to grow. It is already a formidable power for students, within the book factory (or the intellectual production center) that is today's university or college.

We will request funding from the University to set up the desktop publishing facility. This facility will be open for all to use. The Task Force is about self-publishing, and doing so in a collective way, with others. It is not about me publishing you. It is not about you publishing me. Those of us who began this work are aware of the difference between our work process and the standard hierarchical relations in a mainstream book or journal publishing operation. Resources cannot be pooled in a hierarchy. An 'each one teach one' dynamic cannot work in a hierarchy. Our experience is that democracy is a precondition of efficiency and quality production. We all do everything. We do not accept a division of labor, especially between those who have the ideas, who create the stories or do the analysis; and those who labor to get it on the shelf in the form of a book. We know that the dualism of the mind and the body, of men and women, of black and white of manual and intellectual - is also the dualism of hierarchy and exploitation. And because it is the terrain of exploitation it is also the terrain of resistance, of struggle. And the resistance usually takes the form of slow-downs, working to rule, absenteeism, apathy, destruction of resources, theft, and other familiar tactics. We do resist. And the practice of resistance commands support and celebration. But if we can establish the terrain of free action, then we can free ourselves from resistance, from defense, from defensiveness; and engage in real revolution. What is this about? We don't want to spend a lot of time fighting back, especially when we know we have the strength to do what we want to do in an experimental mode, in the womb of the university, and what we do produce will be a powerful example and inspiration to others, suffering anonymous ignomy and being wasted. In short, blow off the hierarchy of exploitation, the dualism of: we women do the shit work, and you men trip off in your castles of acclaim. The bonder is also the bonded. And we know it is a prison to exercise power over each other.

As of early 1989 we are staffing the facility through independent studies (whereby a student gets credits for undertaking a project with a faculty member advising), and on a voluntary basis. Since we have previous experience in desktop publishing, we feel an obligation to teach and consult for those who desire to publish material. As of February 1989 we have as part of the Taskforce activity a weekly newspaper *The Weekly News*, which has more subscribers in three weeks than can be served through photocopies; a syllabus making project in the new junior seminar in Social Thought and Political Economy, a book of poetry, yet another collection of biographies of students' grandmothers, and still more publication projects in the wings. A large number of people are involved. Our experience was presented to a faculty seminar for lecturers who teach writing courses. Over a dozen UMASS writing professors confirmed the importance of democratic relations and commitment in the process of learning to write. The faculty seminar began with a plea to publish within departments. This was presented as a value in itself and as a means of encouraging students to be the best they can be as writers and published authors.

We intend to spread the technology of desktop publishing internationally. We already have plans to publish material from our contacts in China and Nairobi, Kenya.

We fully understand that our plans hang on the availability of funds. We also know that the money needed to implement a small, but powerful, desktop publishing lab is close to nothing compared to money spent on other contracts by the University.

All of us must also realize that the desktop publishing lab would be a great leap forward and an improvement in the process of our education.

Productivity: the Problem of the Third Millennium

How did we do what we did? We tried democracy. We all tried to be egalitarian. We tried to deal with power in relationships between teacher and student and among students, whether male or female, more or less competent, or with more or less time free to work. Consensus works. Democracy and quick action go together. We were together a whole year by the time we put out *Revolutionary Popular Culture* and the democratic practice made us very efficient.

Each of us has many skills, a broad network, access to technology and specialized contacts. Each of us is linked into organizations, affinity groups, waged jobs and networks of many descriptions. We drew on all of these assets. This vast array of resources became socialized and thus at the disposal of the project. We had an unspoken openness about all parts of the project.

We did speak about the priority of process over product. It was more important that something was done in an agreeable way than that it get done. If men tended to control parts of the editing or publishing process because men had computer skills; we went slower so women